WHEN YOUR SOUL ACHES

LOIS MOWDAY RABEY

WHEN

YOUR

SOUL

ACHES

HOPE AND HELP *for* WOMEN
WHO HAVE LOST THEIR HUSBANDS

WATERBROOK
PRESS

WHEN YOUR SOUL ACHES
PUBLISHED BY WATERBROOK PRESS
2375 Telstar Drive, Suite 160
Colorado Springs, Colorado 80920
A division of Random House, Inc.

ISBN 1-57856-144-2

Published in association with the literary agency of Alive Communications, Inc., 7680 Goddard Street, Suite 200, Colorado Springs, Colorado 80920.

Library of Congress Cataloging-in-Publication Data
Rabey, Lois Mowday.
    When your soul aches : hope and help for women who have lost their husbands / by Lois Mowday Rabey.—1st ed.
        p. cm.
    ISBN 1-57856-144-2
        1. Widows—Life skills guides. 2. Widows—Religious life. I. Title.

HQ1058 .R33 2000
305.48'9654—dc21   00-035941

Printed in the United States of America
2000—First Edition

10 9 8 7 6 5 4 3 2 1

For all women who have suffered the loss of a spouse,

with special love to

ELSIE MILLER

CONTENTS

Section Two: "Are There Things I Should Be Doing?"

Section Three: "Should I Be Feeling This Way?"

PART II: WHEN YOU'RE READY
TO MOVE AHEAD

ACKNOWLEDGMENTS

I've had the privilege of working with the same people on several book projects. Familiarity doesn't lessen my gratitude for the assistance and care I continue to receive from these competent writing and publishing professionals: Kathy Yanni, Liz Heaney, and all the people at WaterBrook Press.

To the Tuesday morning ladies group—you are the greatest! Thank you for your prayers and cheerleading: Carol Donaldson, Cathy Eskew, Lynn Ganz, Judi Shive, Susan Wyatt, and Jan Zimmerman.

To my family, all of whom continually encourage and support me—you are bright lights in my life and bring me joy beyond what you could possibly know. Thank you!

And a special thank-you to all the widows I have met with over the years. You know who you are, and you remember, along with me, the times we sat and talked and cried together. Your openness and courage have been an ongoing encouragement to me. I pray that you are continually blessed with God's hope and love.

My Story, Your Story

I have been where you are: widowed, sad, angry, shocked, frightened, comforted, hopeful, lost…confused. I know how alone you can feel.

My first husband, Jack, died more than twenty years ago, but I remember well the day of his death. That event has affected my life ever since.

It was December 15, 1979. Our daughters, Lisa and Lara, and I had purchased a ride in a hot-air balloon as a Christmas present for Jack. We were all excited, and the girls had even managed to keep quiet about the big secret!

The south Florida morning was clear and crisp, a perfect morning for the balloon launch. I had invited two of Jack's close friends and business associates, Glenn Berg and Rick Rhine, to join him on this adventure. After gathering at our house early in the morning and rousting Jack from sleep, Glenn and Rick piled into our station wagon along with our family, Glenn's wife, Gail, and Rick's fiancée, Kathy, and we headed to suburban Fort Lauderdale.

In short order we were at the launch site and the balloon was ready for takeoff. The girls and I waved excitedly from below as the three men and the pilot ascended. We snapped pictures and hurriedly climbed back into the car to follow the balloon. The girls and I were exhilarated. Then it happened. Sheer joy disintegrated into sheer horror in a matter of seconds when the balloon hit power lines and a flame shot out from the side of the basket. I pushed Lisa and Lara down to the floor of the front seat of the car to shield them from the horrifying scene. I watched in disbelief as two men jumped from the burning basket. The balloon rose dramatically as the flames heated the air. Two more people fell before the roaring fire consumed the remains of the wicker basket.

I raced from the car and knelt first beside Glenn's body, not knowing where Jack's had landed. For a few mysterious and unexplainable moments, I felt only peace and the comfort of God's presence. I had no fear or dread or even pain. In that moment God miraculously wrapped me in his arms and showered me with a glimpse of heaven.

God was present in a real and comforting way at this terrible moment, and I knew he would continue to be with us. His tender ministrations would carry me through the early trials of widowhood. They did not erase the pain and struggle, but they gave me hope. No matter what the future held for my children and me, I believed we would not be alone.

My loss was shockingly sudden. Jack and I were both thirty-four years old and in excellent health when he was killed. We had anticipated many long years together.

Was your loss also sudden? Was your husband the victim of an accident, a sudden heart attack, an unexpected stroke? Or did he suffer through the long agony of a terminal illness?

Regardless of the circumstances surrounding your husband's death, the result is the same. Your husband has died. You are a widow. I was a widow. Each of our situations is personal—unique—and yet we share the experience of loss. I want you to know that you are not alone on this journey.

My heart longs to comfort and encourage you, to validate your feelings, and to bring you hope for the days ahead. I have sat at many a kitchen table with other widows as we've cried and laughed together. We have spoken in hushed tones about feelings only we can understand. We have prayed. We have sat in silence. We have shared a sweet communion with each other.

I've tried to capture the essence of those conversations within the pages of this book. I have included other insights as well, insights that might have helped me had I known them when I first became a widow. Part 1 addresses the immediate feelings and needs we face in the early days of loss. Every widow I talk with wants to know: "Why did this happen? Will I always feel this way? Are there things I should be doing? Am I going to get through this?" Part 2 looks ahead to the time when you will be ready to move on and to forge a new future for yourself and your children.

All of the stories in this book are from my own life or from the experiences of widows who agreed to let me tell their stories. Some of the women were young when they lost their husbands, some older. Each entry stands alone, and they can be read in any order.

I pray that your heart will find healing as you wander through these pages.

Part I

In the Early Days of Loss

"Will I Always Hurt This Deeply?"

ONE STEP AT A TIME

Are you asking yourself *Will I make it through this?* Most widows do. Your life has been turned upside down, and the adjustments are daunting. For months after Jack's death, I carried around a seemingly endless to-do list on a yellow legal pad, but that list covered only what needed to be done to settle Jack's business affairs. It didn't address things that needed to be done concerning the kids, the house, the cars, or the finances.

The early days after loss can be overwhelming. You'll hear conflicting advice. You'll have difficulty making decisions about things that seem simple, let alone decisions that are complex or involve matters foreign to you. Some of the best advice I received in those tumultuous days was to slow down and wait on God to give me direction.

A missionary friend's story of a South American tribe illustrates this principle. For some reason, this group moved about only at night. Because they lived in a rugged area that was dotted with steep cliffs, their nighttime journeys were dangerous. But they solved their dilemma by carrying makeshift lanterns that cast just enough light to see one step ahead. As long as they walked slowly and kept their eyes on the lighted ground, they kept on the path. By walking only one step at a time, they were able to keep from falling off a precipice.

Some days you may feel like you are moving through a similarly threatening land. You'll feel lost and afraid of taking a misstep. But if you move slowly and keep your eyes on God, he will help you make wise choices. Take time to consider and evaluate the advice you are given. Spend time with God, asking his specific direction for each step you take. He promises to be with you and to guide you.

> *Show me your ways, O LORD,*
> *teach me your paths;*
> *guide me in your truth and teach me,*
> *for you are God my Savior,*
> *and my hope is in you all day long.*
>
> PSALM 25:4-5

"WHEN WILL LIFE GET BACK TO NORMAL?"

From the morning of Jack's accident until the evening of the memorial service, friends, neighbors, and out-of-town guests steadily flowed through my home. I had to make the funeral arrangements, plan the memorial service, and meet with the many people who supported and comforted the girls and me.

Five days after Jack died, the flurry of activity simply stopped. Only a few close friends remained. Most people had to get back to their jobs and families and things to do; they had to get back to life as normal. I had to go to Jack's office and meet with attorneys and insurance agents. Jack had operated his own insurance agency, and Glenn and Rick were the only agents who worked with him. The accident had wiped out the entire agency at once, leaving me with a huge mess to untangle.

As I drove over to the office that day, I thought, *I'll get this meeting out of the way, and then get back to normal.* But eight hours and sixteen yellow legal-pad pages later, I realized "normal" wouldn't be happening for a long time.

Are you, too, wondering when life will seem normal again?

In the early days of loss, there is little in your life that qualifies as normal. Everything revolves around your loss. You have to attend to legal matters regarding your husband's business affairs and establish yourself as the responsible party for your family. Every day you will be faced with new decisions about your children, your home, your finances, your car, and more. Many of these practical matters are addressed in this book. Try to remember that the feeling of being drowned by changes will subside.

You will feel out-of-joint for a long time. That's okay. In time you will adjust. You will feel normal again, but *normal* won't look the same as before. It will be a new kind of normal.

> *Be strong and take heart, all you who hope in the* Lord.
>
> Psalm 31:24

"What Did He Feel?"

I didn't see Jack's body after the accident, but the coroner's report detailed the cause of death. As I held the lengthy document in my hands, an attorney who was with me suggested that I might not want to read it.

"Tell me what you think his last moments were like," I asked the attorney. He told me that Jack's hands had been badly burned which probably meant that he held on until he passed out, never even being aware that he was falling.

For weeks I played a horrific scene over and over again in my mind. I would look at the burners on the stove and imagine holding my hands on the red-hot coils until I passed out. It was torture.

Then one day I asked a close family friend who is a doctor to explain to me what it might have been like for Jack in the midst of that much pain and panic. My friend gently and reassuringly told me that the body has mechanisms that override pain in life and death situations. In my simplistic understanding I think he meant that pain is not experienced by someone in that situation the same way it would be for someone just thinking about the situation. We cannot project what terminal pain would feel like because the physiological responses present for the person are not present for us.

Jack was undoubtedly trying to think of a way to survive and that thought allowed him to hold on even though his hands were holding on to a burning material.

I have another friend whose husband died a very painful death as a result of cancer. His last days were agony. She told me that, although she desperately wanted him to be healed, she was relieved when the pain was over for him. She didn't play those last weeks over in her mind but focused on the peace that death brought him.

I think the best way to release the torturing mental images of a loved one's last moments is to remember that they were not only experiencing physical responses that we can't imagine, but that they were also the recipients of supernatural grace that carried them from this world to the next.

⟡

SCENT OF A MEMORY

Long before aromatherapy was popular, I loved fragrances. I've worn perfume since I was a young girl, and I've loved the smell of aftershave and men's cologne since sniffing my father's familiar bottle of Old Spice.

Jack wore an aftershave called Royal Copenhagen. Its crystal-blue liquid came in a clear bottle with a blue-and-silver cap. He would pour a small amount into his cupped hand, clap his hands together, and then lightly slap both sides of his face as droplets splashed onto the bathroom countertop. Sometimes he'd quietly come up behind me; I'd get a whiff of Royal Copenhagen and know he was there. The handle on his leather briefcase held traces of that fragrance. When I ironed his shirts, the steam from his collars brought his scent into my presence even though he wasn't there.

After Jack's death I savored those moments when I would capture his scent from his clothes or briefcase. And after I took his clothes out of the closet and put his briefcase in storage, I'd sometimes sprinkle drops of Royal Copenhagen from his half-used bottle onto my pillowcase. I'd bury my head in the pillow and inhale deeply. And then I'd cry for a long time.

In the days ahead, many things will remind you of your husband. Don't be afraid to embrace them. You need to remember him and your life together. Good memories can be healing.

"AFTER FORTY-FIVE YEARS, HE'S GONE"

Elsie lost her husband of forty-five years after a brief bout with cancer. Her five grown sons and their families are spread across the country from the East Coast to the West Coast, and she is in the midland of Missouri. She is grateful for frequent contact with her children and grandchildren, but she talked to me of the strangeness that accompanies the loss of a lifetime mate. "I really miss having someone to care if I had a good day or to tell news to or to talk things over with. It's hard, too, coping with a couples' world and not fitting in with anybody."

As she told me how difficult the weekends are, particularly Sundays, I remembered all too well that isolated feeling when sitting in a church pew surrounded by other families. Elsie had spent nearly a half-century sitting next to the same man in church and listening to him sing a solo or preach a sermon. She told me, "It's difficult, but my hope is that I can minister to other women who have lost a husband. I want to be a good witness to the fact that God is in control of my situation."

The loss of a spouse after so many years not only leaves a huge emotional void, but also prompts changes in a long-established lifestyle. Over the years two people become so connected that the death of one leaves the other adrift. Elsie, like other women who have lost a spouse later in life, is moving on. She still hurts, but she is coping and growing.

If you have lost a life partner, hang on to hope. Like Elsie, you will survive. Your pain will lessen. You will experience joy again.

"When will the pain go away?" Julie asked me. Her husband had died suddenly, leaving her with an infant and a toddler to rear alone.

"I'm afraid all of the pain doesn't go away," I answered softly. "But it does lessen, and peace increases."

Julie thought that God's peace meant the absence of pain. She believed that if she could just do enough of the right spiritual things, she would find comfort and no longer feel the pain of loss.

Scripture never promises Christians a pain-free life. Instead, the Bible is filled with words and phrases like *perseverance, endurance, finishing the race,* and *standing firm to the end,* and we miss their implication. Life involves pain—that's why we need perseverance, endurance, and encouragement to keep on keeping on. But in the midst of our deepest pain, God's inexpressible peace invades our hearts and brings us joy in the sorrow.

As the years pass, you will experience more joy and less pain, but the loose threads of grief will come up every now and then, reminding you of your loss. Fourteen years after Jack died, my daughter Lara married. She and Craig were married in southern California on a beautiful, sunny day in mid-December. The bridal party arrived at the church several hours before the ceremony to take pictures. Lara and her bridesmaids had dressed in one of the parlor rooms of the church amid a flurry of girl-talk and makeup. They had moved outside for photos in the courtyard, and I had stayed behind to make sure nothing essential was left behind.

As I came out of the dressing room, I saw Lara posed for the camera. Suddenly she flinched and broke her pose; tears spilled down her face. Just then, I saw her Uncle Bud, who bears a striking resemblance to Jack, walk up and hug her. Neither of them said a word. They smiled and cried, looking at each other knowingly.

That poignant moment held both peace and pain. In that moment a daughter and a brother shared the pain of loss and the absolute joy of Lara's wedding. The pain didn't ruin the day, nor did it diminish the peace. And the very touch of God transformed the pain into peace.

No, pain doesn't completely go away this side of heaven, so there's no point in trying to run from it. Accept it and ask God to touch those deeply painful places of your soul with his love.

Because of the tender mercy of our God,
by which the rising sun will come to us from
heaven
to shine on those living in darkness
and in the shadow of death,
to guide our feet into the path of peace.

LUKE 1:78-79

"My Husband Made All the Decisions"

"I was a 1950s kind of wife," Betty told me. "Even though John and I did everything together, he made all the final decisions. I don't say this in a detrimental way. I loved the thirty-eight years when I didn't have to make the decisions."

The loss of her lifelong companion forced Betty into a steep learning curve. "I'm learning accounting, how to buy and sell a car, how to invest in mutual funds, how to hire and manage people to work on my house and car. I didn't do any of these things before. I have to decide how much money is enough to live on, do I stay in the house or move, and if I move, where?"

Betty's first six months of widowhood were horrible, and she found herself in a deep pit of hopelessness. "It was terrible to see the empty chair where John would have sat, to eat alone. An intense loneliness and despair almost swallowed me. Then I made a decision that changed my despair to hope. I decided to let God walk me through this, and I began to move one step at a time. I chose to not be bitter." Today Betty facilitates grief workshops and is involved in ministry at her church. Her pain no longer consumes her.

It's doubly overwhelming to lose a husband and simultaneously to be faced with decisions you have never wrestled with on your own. Make an intentional decision to believe that you will live through this. Allow God to come next to you and show you the way. Ask him to fill you with hope and a desire to live well as a woman full of life.

> *You are my hiding place;*
> *you will protect me from trouble*
> *and surround me with songs of deliverance.*
>
> PSALM 32:7

No "Right" Way to Grieve

Americans subscribe to an unwritten rule that says mourning should last a year, and then our hearts should be healed. I was told that once I had gone through our anniversary, Jack's birthday, and all the major holidays, I would feel much better. Not true! Some days *were* better, but others were painful…for a long time.

Grief resists all labels. It isn't linear. We don't progress neatly from one stage of grief to the next. Grief is messy, bewildering, and encompasses a range of emotions. I would feel easily excited one moment and down in the dumps the next. Just when I felt I had overcome some fear, it would sneak back into my thinking.

Your journey through grief is unique. Many of the thoughts you read in this book will express exactly how you feel. Others will seem foreign. That's okay. There isn't a "right" way to grieve. It is a process, but it is an individual process. So in the days ahead, feel what you feel and don't be concerned if your experience differs from that of others.

DENIAL IS NORMAL

Many years ago, one of Jack's friends from helicopter flight school was killed in Vietnam. His body was never recovered, and only his dog tags were returned to his widow. Jack was a pallbearer at the funeral. At the graveside the widow threw herself on the coffin and begged for someone to open it so she could see her husband, but there was no body to show her. Her tears and pleadings filled the air with her pain. She wanted some evidence of her husband's death so that she could really believe it. How I ached for her!

Many women experience denial, even those who are present at the time of death. Denial gives you time to adjust to the wrenching loss of your spouse. Intellectually you know your husband has died, but emotionally that reality is too horrifying to embrace right away. That's okay. You may have moments when you expect your husband to walk in the door any minute. Or you may dream that your husband is still alive or that he didn't *really* die in the accident or in the hospital.

But denial can be unhealthy if it becomes a way of life. If you act as if your husband is still alive—talking to him, pretending he is with you, living in a fantasy—you may need professional help. Check with your pastor for a referral to a Christian counselor or with friends who may know someone to recommend. Also check with churches in your area to see if any offer grief workshops you could attend.

Denial is normal. It comes and goes, and in time it disappears completely.

"Where Is My Husband When I Need Him?"

Math frustrates me, so Jack always balanced our books. When he was gone, I had to learn to balance them myself. I put if off as long as I could.

Finally, I sat at the dining room table with bills and papers spread in front of me. Lisa and Lara were tucked into bed, and I had planned to balance the checkbook for the first time in my life. I gave myself what I thought was a reasonable amount of time to follow the steps listed on the back of my latest statement. It wasn't long before I was fuming. My figures just didn't match the bank's balance. I worked through the steps again. Still a significant discrepancy.

"Where are you, Jack! I need you!" I said loudly. I was angry—angry that he left me, angry that I had to do something I hated and couldn't do well, angry that my days of having a partner to share the load were over. I was angry with Jack for dying and leaving me alone.

I knew my ire was futile, and it didn't last long. But I felt it, expressed it out loud, laughed at myself, and then attacked the checkbook again. I never did reconcile the figures that evening. The next day I went to the bank and found a sympathetic person who balanced the account for me and showed me how to do it.

Every widow I've met has been angry at her husband for dying and leaving her alone, even though her husband didn't choose to die, didn't desert her in the usual sense of the word, didn't actually do anything to incur her wrath. But she is angry with him anyway.

Many of us are also angry with God. We are angry that God allowed this tragedy to happen. We are mad because he didn't intervene. He could have, so why didn't he? Such questions, asked sincerely, can lead to healing. God receives our anger and returns love. We often feel better after we've vented.

If you feel anger bubbling out of your frustration and pain, let it out. Don't let it build. Get it out and clear the way for God's touch of love to come in and calm you.

The LORD longs to be gracious to you;
he rises to show you compassion.
For the LORD is a God of justice.
Blessed are all who wait for him!

ISAIAH 30:18

If Only...

The girls and I gave Jack, Glenn, and Rick the balloon ride as a present. They died as a result of our gift. I can't count the number of times I thought, *If only we hadn't bought that balloon ride...*

The words *if only* often haunt those of us who are left behind. These words produce guilt and generate deep feelings of remorse and regret. Even if we don't feel guilt about circumstances surrounding the death, we usually feel guilt over unsaid words or words said in anger. We wish we'd done something differently.

We seem to think that if we could live our marriage over, we would live it perfectly. In reality, we all make mistakes, say things that hurt others, and miss opportunities to be loving and affirming.

But, you may be thinking, *I did some spiteful things that I would take back if I only had the chance. I do regret my attitude toward my husband a lot of the time.* If this is the case, you may need to ask God's forgiveness and then forgive yourself.

Though you can't turn back the clock, you can improve the relationships you are in today. You can learn from mistakes and grow as a result. Let yourself grieve the things you wish you had done differently, learn from them, and forgive yourself.

What's Your Way of Coping?

I responded to the unexpected—and unwanted—responsibilities that used to be Jack's by charging ahead. I felt more in control when I was busy, so I plowed on. My activity carried its own set of challenges: I sometimes made decisions too quickly; I often ran on adrenaline and then crashed; and I neglected my need to take time to grieve and take care of myself. My life was out of balance, but I wasn't about to let grief get me down!

Fortunately, I had people around me who cautioned me to slow down. They advised me not to make major decisions—like selling the house or moving—for at least a year. They reminded me that I needed to spend both quantity and quality time with my children. They encouraged me to pace myself and to give my body, mind, and spirit time to heal and be restored.

Some women who are overwhelmed with grief respond in the opposite way. Instead of filling their lives with action, they stay in bed. The painful emotions of widowhood eventually overpower them, and they become chronically depressed.

If determination to survive keeps you busy, busy, busy, running on adrenaline—take a breath. Stop and evaluate your pace. Talk with some friends about how to moderate your activity so it's healthy, allowing time for your family, your health, and your spiritual nourishment.

If you can't get out of bed, handle even the smallest of life's chores, or think clearly, enlist the help of your friends. Ask them to help you find a counselor or grief recovery group. Invite your friends to walk through this journey with you. If you don't have anyone in your life who can walk alongside you and lend support, then call some churches and ask about support groups for widows. This may sound risky, but you will heal much more quickly with the help of others.

❧

One Day, You'll Feel Ready to Move On

On November 4, 1979, fifty-two Americans were taken hostage when Iranian militants stormed the U.S. Embassy in Teheran. Newspapers and television offered daily accounts of their continuing ordeal. People tied yellow ribbons around trees, mailboxes, and light posts—any object they could—across the front yards of America. Jack and I followed the story and prayed for the safe return of the hostages. Every day we listened to the radio and television reports and scanned the newspapers for updates.

One day in May after Jack's death, I opened the newspaper and was surprised to see a story about the hostages. I had not read one newspaper or tuned in to a single television show since Jack's death on December 15, and I had forgotten all about the hostages. Grief and responsibility had consumed me. I had nothing left for anyone or anything outside my immediate family. Our loss had absorbed all my thoughts and feelings. Even the biggest news story of the day had escaped my notice.

I didn't feel guilty, but I did sense a desire to reconnect, to emerge from my cocoon.

In the months ahead, you will be absorbed with your loss. Don't feel badly about this. Your feelings are normal. There is no prescribed timetable for grief. Eventually you will want to reconnect with others; in time your ache will lessen and you will begin to heal.

> *Weeping may remain for a night, but rejoicing comes in the morning.*
>
> PSALM 30:5

"Are There Things I Should Be Doing?"

PRAY

When I first became a widow, prayer took on a fresh meaning. Instead of setting aside a specific time to pray, I prayed throughout the day, constantly conversing with God about what I was feeling or experiencing. Stripped of any illusion of self-sufficiency, I was deeply aware that I needed God's help with everything from breathing to buying cars. Prayer became not only a holy endeavor, but also a necessary ingredient in learning to live with God as my husband.

How else could I survive, let alone make wise decisions?

Ironically, when people ask what they can do to help, many widows reply, "All you can do is pray," as if prayer is of lesser value than cooking meals or driving carpools. Sometimes this answer comes from a heart that is aware of our absolute dependence on God for everything, and other times it comes from a sense of exasperation that we are not in control of our lives. It's as if prayer is the ugly stepsister on our list of significant helps. Yet prayer is the most practical thing you can do to guide you through this maze of widowhood.

If you realize, for example, that some important bill has inadvertently gone unpaid, don't panic, pray. Prayer can't write the check and satisfy the creditor, but prayer can give you the presence of mind to deal with the situation.

If you can't find the title to your husband's pickup and can't transfer the truck to your name without it, don't panic, pray. Prayer won't make the title pop out of its hiding place in the files, but prayer can give you the calmness to assess the situation and let options occur to you. Perhaps you'll be inspired to call the Department of Motor Vehicles for assistance. Or perhaps a friend can tell you how to obtain an official copy.

Be assured that God hears your prayers. When you seek him, God offers great comfort and wisdom.

> *"For I know the plans I have for you," declares the*
> *LORD, "plans to prosper you and not to harm you,*
> *plans to give you hope and a future. Then you will*
> *call upon me and come and pray to me, and I will*

listen to you. You will seek me and find me when
you seek me with all your heart."

JEREMIAH 29:11-13

GO AHEAD AND CREATE A MEMORIAL

I love pictures and have always taken photographs. Numerous albums and boxes of photos document every major event of my life, and many minor ones. Shortly after Jack died, I selected dozens of my favorite pictures of him and had them enlarged: pictures from his high-school and college basketball days, pictures of him in his army reserve uniform, pictures of us together, pictures of him with the girls. These photographs chronicled our life together.

I displayed all of them. Every wall and table in our house had visual reminders of Jack. Anyone who entered the house knew that the man captured so frequently on film was revered, loved, and missed. In those early days, these pictures comforted me. I wanted to see him at every turn. I wanted to remember.

Don't be afraid to remember. Surround yourself with things

that remind you of your husband and of your life together. You can put them away later. For now, display as many as you want.

GETTING RID OF THE BED

About a year before Jack died, we purchased a king-size waterbed. I hadn't wanted one, but Jack was persistent, so I finally relented. Even he agreed it wasn't as blissful as he'd expected. For one thing, our weight difference created a problem for us. We couldn't get the water level adjusted properly. If the water level was too low, we'd roll toward the middle. If it was too high, we'd both rest on top of a slightly rounded surface. We finally settled on a level that allowed both of us to be fairly comfortable. Jack delighted in our sea-worthy cradle, but I did not!

The night of his accident, I couldn't bring myself to sleep alone in our bed. No longer would I roll into him in the middle of the bed or sleep perched on top of the firmer side of the mattress. That first night I slept on the sofa bed in our family room.

It's funny how silly arguments can become the source of great longing. I would have gladly claimed my side of our waterbed if it meant sharing it with Jack again.

Many of the challenges of widowhood have to be met: Children need to be raised, finances handled, cars repaired, yard work tackled. But some challenges can be tossed rather than confronted day after day. I tossed the bed. It reminded me of playful sparring over a mild disagreement that I would have loved to tangle over again.

Is there some possession you need to toss? Don't be hasty, but don't feel you have to keep everything either.

WRITE DOWN COMFORTING SCRIPTURE VERSES

Despite today's technological sophistication, I still use pen or pencil to record my thoughts and experiences. My day-planner has a section of blank pages, which I write in frequently. It's not an electronic-miracle data-keeper, and I like it that way. There is something therapeutic about thoughts moving from my mind, through my fingers, and onto a page.

At the time I became a widow, technology as we know it now was a dream of the future. So if a verse comforted and strengthened me, I wrote it in longhand on an index card and carried it with me. My stack of cards grew so large that I put them in a little metal index box and carried it with me.

I suggest you consider doing the same: Copy by hand the words of God that fill you with hope, joy, and peace and remind you of his love. Write down the words that settle your painful emotions and fill your heart with the evidence that God fulfills his promises.

Many of the verses I recorded professed God's presence with me even when I felt he was far away. As long as I could believe he was really near—despite my feelings—I felt like I would make it through those difficult days. These are a few that comforted me:

> As I was with Moses, so I will be with you; I will never leave you nor forsake you. (Joshua 1:5)

> Keep me as the apple of your eye; hide me in the shadow of your wings. (Psalm 17:8)

> I am still confident of this: I will see the goodness of the LORD in the land of the living. Wait for the LORD; be strong and take heart and wait for the LORD. (Psalm 27:13-14)

Weeping may remain for a night, but rejoicing comes in the morning. (Psalm 30:5)

As it is written: "No eye has seen, no ear has heard, no mind has conceived what God has prepared for those who love him." (1 Corinthians 2:9)

Which verses comfort you? Which ones bring you hope? Write them down and keep them with you. (At the back of this book is an additional list of comforting scriptures.) They will help you claim the truth even when your emotions draw you away from it. Believing what God says makes a difference.

RECORD YOUR FEELINGS

I'd encourage you to make use of a journal as a cathartic tool. Writing down your feelings will help you weave through the tangle of emotions. You will understand yourself better as you put words to your emotions and find relief as you articulate them.

In the intensity of the moment, all of us think we will never forget how we feel or how God is moving on our behalf. But our memories dim as time passes. Journal entries provide a written record of our progress and God's intervention. We can read about yesterday's struggles and compare them with where we are today.

In the early days of widowhood, for example, I wrote down my fears about rearing my children alone. After some weeks had passed, I became aware that I felt more confident as a single parent. I wrote that the girls were adjusting and that we were establishing a fulfilling home, just the three of us. As I looked back through my journal, I could recall the fear, read about the changes in our lives, and see how far I had come from fear to confidence. This written record affirmed my faith. God had heard my cries for help!

Plan a day to go to several stationery stores or bookstores and pick out a lovely blank book in which you can record your feelings. Write anything, everything. Just let it all out—plan, ponder, ramble. If you just hate to write, I can only encourage you to give it a try. Maybe you would prefer to record your feelings and thoughts on a computer. That's okay too.

Widowhood is a dense jungle in the early years. Writing can help you unravel some of the internal tangle by enabling you to think in new ways, see from different perspectives, and grow into the woman God wants you to be.

Give it a try.

Get Your Paperwork Organized ASAP

The morning after Jack's memorial service, I met with attorneys, insurance agents, our pastor, and a financial advisor in Jack's office, now eerily empty. The custodian had been coming in daily and putting all the mail on Jack's desk. It had grown to a precarious pile. The letters on the top had begun to slide off and fall to the floor. I came in and sat in Jack's chair, dwarfed by the paper mountain in front of me. One of the men handed me a yellow legal pad and a pen. "You will need these," he said kindly, "to make a list."

Eight hours and eighteen pages later, I left the office with my to-do list. I felt overwhelmed, but also encouraged by those men who would spend the next year helping me sort out the legalities of closing the agency.

As we were leaving one of them reminded me to go down to the Social Security office and file a claim. Then he added that I should also get copies of the death certificate to send to businesses to inform them that I was assuming responsibility for our accounts: credit cards, the mortgage, the car payment.

I wasn't very organized in those days. I carried my yellow legal pad around and checked things off, but I didn't have a system for filing important papers. I tended to throw everything in a desk drawer, telling myself that someday soon the busywork would end.

But it doesn't.

I encourage you to get organized as soon as possible. If you have problems knowing how to do this, ask for help.

I wish I had. Begin with your friends who are experts in the areas where you are weak. Ask an accountant or bookkeeper to meet with you and help you set up a record-keeping system. If you have a personal computer but are not familiar with using it for record keeping, make a similar arrangement with an experienced computer user. Be respectful of other people's time and offer to pay them. Many people are more than willing to help if they just know you need it.

BECOME AN ADVOCATE FOR YOURSELF

I called the telephone company to ask them to take Jack's name off the bill and put my name on it. Naively, I didn't expect any problems.

"Mrs. Mowday, you will need to send us four hundred dollars to continue your phone service," a woman on the other end of the phone told me matter-of-factly.

"What?" I replied, thinking that I misunderstood her.

"You will have to send us four hundred dollars to continue your phone service."

"Why?" I asked in disbelief.

She explained that I was opening a new account, and because our old telephone bills had run more than several hundred dollars a month, I would have to give the equivalent of a two-month deposit. We had never been late with any payment, and I didn't see how changing the name on our account constituted opening a new account. But she was unmoved. I asked if she could just add the deposit to my next bill, and she said no, and that I would need to send a check in or bring one to the local office in person. I had ten days to do so.

Though shocked and furious, I assumed I had no option but to comply.

A few days later, I received a phone call from the president of the local branch of the telephone company. He apologized profusely and said that no additional deposit would be required. When I asked him what had precipitated the change, he told me that my attorney had called him.

I must have relayed the story to my attorney in the course of a conversation, and he took the initiative to call the phone company on my behalf. My attorney also happened to be a Florida state representative.

"Thank you," I said. "But what happens to the people who don't have a state representative helping them?" There was silence on the other end of the phone. I realized I was being ungracious and apologized.

Businesses, for the most part, may be indifferent to your situation. If you encounter problems when changing the name on any of your bills or accounts, be respectful but firm about what you need. Seek help if you run into demands that seem unusual or that you are unable to meet. You will need to be your own advocate. This does not mean you have to become strident or aggressive, but you will need to be aware and wise.

Be as shrewd as snakes and as innocent as doves.

MATTHEW 10:16

Be Wise and Cautious About Financial Affairs

Before Jack died, I was horribly ignorant about money matters. And I spent too much.

Many widows are provided for financially in their husband's will, giving them excess funds for the first time in their lives. Such a surplus can tempt you to spend more than is prudent, and it makes you vulnerable to the ploys of a money manager or investor who may not be acting in your best interest.

While there are many honest and well-meaning people in financial fields, some will put their own interests above yours. Because some of these people garner names from obituaries, it might be helpful to get an unlisted phone number to avoid a flood of unsolicited calls. Make sure that everyone with whom you do business provides references, and then check them. Friends can be helpful, but friendship can muddy the water of decision making. You may disagree about an investment but feel hesitant to express any reservation because of the friendship.

Managing finances requires discernment and assistance. Whatever your situation, I advise you to be cautious. Take your time before you make any financial decisions. Talk with those close to you who are knowledgeable. Read. Attend seminars, but be aware that many are sponsored by people who hope to sign you on as a client.

A wonderful resource for widows with excess funds is the ministry Royal Treasure. This organization was founded by a good friend of mine, Lu Dunbar, who worked in development with a number of Christian organizations for years. She met regularly with widows who were interested in giving to worthy causes. During the course of many conversations, Lu found that many widows had been taken advantage of financially. They had been ill advised by financial people and sought after by many solicitors looking for donations or investments—secular and Christian.

Royal Treasure offers information and seminars that help educate women on financial matters, with a specific emphasis on women who are making these decisions alone. The organization is located in Atlanta, Georgia. Lu may be contacted by e-mail at LuDunbar@ royaltreasure.org or through her Web site: www.RoyalTreasure.org.

EARN A LIVING

But what if you were not left with adequate resources? If you are in this situation, your challenges are even more pressing. You may need to simplify your lifestyle or enter the workplace, perhaps for the first time or after an absence of many years.

Elaine, a widow in her early forties with three children, found herself in this situation when her husband died suddenly of a heart attack. His small insurance policy barely covered their living expenses for the first year. "Friends and the people at my church really helped out," she said. "They filled the gap until I could get a job, and then they continued to help with baby-sitting."

If you don't have friends or family nearby who can help you through this transition time, consider checking out some local churches where you might be able to get plugged in and receive spiritual, practical, and financial help. Also look in your local newspaper for churches that offer grief workshops and sign up for one. Usually those groups are well informed about available aid.

But don't rely on others as a long-term solution to your financial challenges. Talk with people about finding a job or getting the training or education you need to become marketable. In most larger cities, there are numerous classes for working adults that offer undergraduate and graduate degree programs that adapt to busy schedules. You will also find a variety of vocationally specific training courses that may suit your needs. Many of these are offered at a reasonable cost; check with your state department of education.

No matter how overwhelming this all sounds, you can navigate the challenges one step at a time. Begin where you are. Start talking, inquiring, listening, believing you can make a living, and moving toward this goal.

Eat Well

I couldn't eat anything solid for days after Jack died. A smorgasbord of food flowed into our home, but I couldn't get anything down. My only "nourishment" was coffee. Then one day something actually smelled inviting. One of my friends was heating a clear broth on the stove and told me that Nancy had delivered the soup earlier that day. The mild fragrance enticed me to accept a bowl, and I slowly sipped the warm liquid.

Someone commented that of all the wonderful, fancy foods that had come into the house, I had chosen the simplest. "Yes," I said, "and look who knew what to bring."

Nancy had lost a child some years before. She knew what it was like to almost gag when thinking about forcing solid food down your constricted throat. I felt a kinship with her and smiled at her sweet gift of a simple broth that nourished my soul as well as my body.

Your normal pattern of eating has undoubtedly been disrupted. You may be inclined to be obsessive either by eating too little or too much. Try to eat just a few sensible foods as you get through the early days. After a while you will again have the desire to eat well.

GET A PHYSICAL

About six months into my widowhood, some friends and I were talking one day about a stress test that had appeared in a women's magazine. One of the ladies had a copy of the test and gave it to me. I took it home and filled it out that night.

The test assigned points to different life events, and these points were an indicator of the amount of stress each event could produce. The article said that if you scored over three hundred points, you were considered in serious peril for stress-related maladies. I scored seven hundred points. Within a year, in addition to facing Jack's death, my father was diagnosed with cancer, my parents moved, and our dog died—and those were just the major stressors!

At the urging of my friends, I scheduled a routine physical. The doctor was kind and understanding, and he confirmed that it is a good idea to have a physical examination when you have been under so much emotional stress. All turned out to be well, and he even gave me a dispensation with regard to drinking coffee. He told me he felt it would be more stressful to ask me to quit than to allow me to continue one of my most pleasurable indulgences.

Even if you have no symptoms of illness, get a physical sometime within the first year of widowhood. If you have some specific concerns, such as insomnia, nervousness, anxiety, or weight gain or loss, be sure to mention them to your doctor.

FIND A HANDYMAN

We were remodeling our home when Jack died. He had been doing much of the work himself, so I was at a loss as to how to finish what he had started. Baseboards were off, walls were unpainted, and electrical work was incomplete.

I called several people listed in the phone book, but most declined to take on small, wrap-up jobs that someone else had started. One day some friends from church were visiting, and the husband looked around in dismay. When he realized that I had a number of unfinished jobs to be done around the house, he offered to help. He said that if I could be patient, he would try to work in the things I needed around his other jobs. I was so grateful that I leaped at his offer.

When the girls and I moved to Colorado, I found myself in the same predicament. We built a house, but when it was finished, I was unable to stay ahead of the repairs. This time another single woman referred me to a handyman. I hired him to hang outside Christmas lights, haul trash to the dump, and haul and stack wood. He did all sorts of odd jobs for me and proved invaluable.

Maybe you are very handy yourself and don't need such a person, but if not, put the word out with friends and at church. Visit your local hardware store and let them know you are looking for someone to help with odd jobs. Lots of people make a good living doing this and will be a great help to you. When inquiring, don't broadcast that you are living alone. Simply state that you are looking for help.

Take Safety Precautions

Vicki had been widowed about six months when the first letter arrived. She didn't recognize the handwriting, and there was no return address. The scrawled words were difficult to read, but as she deciphered them, she began to feel threatened. An unknown voyeur was writing to let her know that she and her children were being watched.

A very frightened Vicki continued to receive mail from this person for the next few months. All attempts to discover the writer failed. She got an unlisted number, installed an alarm system, and was diligent about locking doors. Eventually the letters stopped, but Vicki's sense of vulnerability lingered.

Single women can be targets for unwanted advances or attention. Lock your doors even if you live in a community where unlocked doors are the norm. Teach your children commonsense rules of safety. Don't become an alarmist, but do become careful. Combine wisdom about the world with your trust in God's watchful care.

"Should I Be Feeling This Way?"

"Why Did This Happen?"

We had a joint memorial service for Jack and the two friends who died with him. Because we all belonged to a large church, and because of the extensive news coverage of the accident, some people had to sit in an overflow section. A number who came didn't know the Lord. We were told later that many of those people accepted Christ as a result of the testimonies of these three men.

Even in death, those three lives influenced others to come to Christ. God truly blessed and comforted all of us with this good news.

Yet my primary question remained unanswered: *Why?* I was happy that people accepted Christ that day, but I also knew that God could have brought them to salvation another way. He could have intervened in the chain of events that led to these three deaths and, at the same time, brought those same people at the memorial service to a knowledge of himself in some other way.

If God had given me a choice between Jack's life and the lives of those people, I wouldn't have hesitated to choose Jack.

Why didn't God intervene and allow him and his two friends to live longer?

I don't believe we could ever find a reason that would satisfy us. Any explanation would still raise the question, *Why not do it differently, God?*

I have never faced a greater test of my faith than this. Would I keep demanding an answer that made sense or would I accept that God is both loving and all-powerful? Would I trust that God loves me? That he cares about me and Jack and our girls?

We can't explain why Christians suffer and die. Oh, we might be able to explain it theologically. We can say that all pain is the result of sin—if not our own, then Adam's. But we don't think it's fair that we should suffer because of something Adam did. And even so, the doctrine of sin doesn't explain why sometimes God intervenes and other times he doesn't.

While your "whys" may never be answered, it is possible to accept the paradox of God's sovereign love and his allowance of pain. Ask for the grace to live with unanswered questions and to relax in the comfort of gratitude when that grace flows into your life.

Oh, the depth of the riches of the wisdom and knowledge of God! How unsearchable his judgments, and his paths beyond tracing out!

ROMANS 11:33

"I'M SO ANGRY!"

"Sometimes I am so angry," Marie said to me, "and I know I shouldn't feel this way."

"Why not?" I asked.

"It isn't godly," she replied.

Marie and I talked about the feelings that flood us when we are adjusting to the loss of a spouse. At times we feel peace and comfort, and at other times we feel anger, fear, and doubt. And then we feel guilty, especially if we believe that Christians are supposed to be free from any negative emotions.

But emotions aren't right or wrong, good or bad. They are natural, human responses to the events and circumstances of life. The death of a spouse is a traumatic event that produces mixed emotions, many of them negative. But we can find healing in the experience and expression of negative feelings.

Jesus modeled emotional honesty with himself and God regarding his crucifixion. Scripture tells us that the night of his arrest: "He withdrew about a stone's throw beyond them, knelt down and prayed, 'Father, if you are willing, take this cup from me; yet not my will, but yours be done'" (Luke 22:41-42). Like Jesus, we can express our grief or anger. At the same time, like Jesus, we can accept the will of God for us.

There were days when I felt I should be "over" Jack's death, days when I wanted to forget about my feelings and get on with my life. But by God's grace I was surrounded by friends who kept reminding me that healing comes when we accept and embrace what we feel. They encouraged me to invite God into my healing. And I urge you to do the same.

Be honest about your feelings, and put yourself in God's hands. Express how you feel, grieve, and weep. Ask for God's healing and continue to wrestle with a confluence of emotions.

GUILT ABOUT FEELING GOOD

I met with Connie a few months after her husband had died from a heart attack. She greeted me warmly as we slid into a booth at a local restaurant. Before we even ordered, Connie looked cautiously over her shoulder, then leaned across the table. "I have been so eager to talk to you," she whispered. "I don't think anyone else could understand what I want to talk to you about." Connie began to pour out her feelings with a mixture of joy and guilt. "I have a fair number of days when I feel—well, good!"

Connie was aware that people sometimes see a widow's lifted spirits and wonder, *Doesn't she miss her husband? Has she forgotten him so quickly? Is she glad he's gone? Is she seeing another man already?* Ironically, these same people were probably praying that Connie would be comforted!

There will be days when you feel good—thank God for them. They are evidence that God heals in miraculous ways. Good days offer tangible hope that you really will live through this difficult time.

When you begin to feel better, give God the credit and don't worry about what other people think.

Praise be to the God and Father of our Lord Jesus Christ! In his great mercy he has given us new birth into a living hope through the resurrection of Jesus Christ from the dead, and into an inheritance that can never perish, spoil or fade—kept in heaven for you, who through faith are shielded by God's power until the coming of the salvation that is ready to be revealed in the last time.

1 PETER 1:3-5

TIME DOESN'T HEAL ALL WOUNDS

When people quote the maxim that time heals all wounds, they mean that if we just wait long enough the pain will go away. But that is not true. The pain lessens, but it never goes away completely.

Just this past week I again felt the pain of losing Jack as I sat in the stands at a state basketball tournament. My older daughter, Lisa, is the assistant coach for the girls' varsity basketball team at the same school where she played basketball a decade ago, and I had come to cheer her team on.

It was exciting to be back in the super-charged setting of high-school basketball play-offs. As the band played and the cheerleaders yelled, I was transported back to my own high-school days when I cheered for another star basketball player—the star that I would one day marry.

And thirteen short years later, he was taken from me.

I still feel pain every now and then. The pain is not as deep as it once was and it doesn't last as long, but it's there, a reminder that the loose threads of grief wisp around us for many years after our loss.

I have known some widows who suffer greatly many years after their loss because they don't allow God to touch them, to heal them. Instead of easing the pain, the passing years only prove to make them increasingly bitter.

Don't let that happen to you.

Healing does not mean we will experience no further pain. But your Father can comfort you. Stay close to him—always. He is the Great Physician. He wants you to have abundant life no matter what your circumstances, and he can bring healing that results in that abundance.

> *I have come that they may have life, and have it to the full.*
>
> JOHN 10:10

"God, Where Are You?"

Loneliness. It's the most painful part of losing your husband. You miss him specifically, and you miss the intimate companionship of another human being. Even the most introverted of us longs for close connection: to know and be known, to be accepted, to be understood. In human relationships, a healthy, loving marriage is the most likely relationship for this kind of intimacy to grow. When that relationship is gone, an enormous vacuum is created.

While children, friends, and family can help fill that void, only God can fill the emptiness. Recently I spoke to a group of singles about loneliness. After my opening talk, a woman raised her hand. She had tried to spend time with God to help her with her loneliness, she said, but she didn't feel his presence. "What do you do when you call out to God and there is silence?" she asked.

I wish I had an easy answer. I don't. Sensing God's presence takes time and persistence and faith. We relate to God in a different way than we do to each other. We don't see him with our eyes or hear him with our ears or touch him with our hands. We relate to God on a spiritual level, but that doesn't mean that he isn't present with us. He tells us that nothing can separate us from him, from his presence: "And surely I am with you always, to the very end of the age" (Matthew 28:20).

I love this passage of Scripture: "And I pray that you, being rooted and established in love, may have power, together with all the saints, to grasp how wide and long and high and deep is the love of Christ, and to know this love that surpasses knowledge— that you may be filled to the measure of all the fullness of God" (Ephesians 3:17-19). I want to know more of this love!

Sometimes I think that the best we can do is to just keep reminding ourselves that God is present, standing next to me, next to you. We can remember these verses, call him by name, and wait. If there is silence, we reaffirm what we know to be true. Like children, we trust that he does not leave us alone and forsaken.

When my grandson Justin had just learned to walk, I was baby-sitting him one day at his house. He was standing by his toy chest, and I was sitting on the sofa, reading a magazine. After a while, I got up and went into the kitchen to get a drink. As I opened the refrigerator, I noticed that it had gotten quiet in the living room. Before I could call to him, Justin called to me.

"Nana!" he cried out in an anxious voice.

"I'm right here, honey," I quickly replied, "in the kitchen." I could hear his little feet pattering across the living-room carpet as he ran to me. He threw his arms around my knees and held on tight.

Just because you can't see God doesn't mean he isn't present. God is with you all the time. You may not be aware of him or you may feel that he is far off, but he is near. When you are troubled, stop and, like a child, call out the name of Jesus. Wait long enough for his spirit to touch yours with the assurance of his presence. Believe he is with you even if you can't feel his nearness.

"HOW CAN I EVER TRUST AGAIN?"

One day shortly after Jack died, I was walking out of the house to pick up the girls at school. The phone rang, and I ran back in to answer it. The call was brief, but I was still a few minutes late to pick up Lisa and Lara. When I arrived they were waiting for me with anxious tears in their eyes.

"Where have you been, Mom?" they cried.

"I just took a phone call. I'm not that late."

While I tried to minimize their fear, I understood it. Even today, twenty years after Jack's accident, I'm fearful when my children are late in meeting me and when they are traveling on a plane or driving in a storm.

When someone you love dies unexpectedly or tragically, you can no longer say, "That will never happen to me." You can no longer bet that the odds are in your favor; the odds have already beaten you. As a widow you hold this awareness in tandem with the knowledge that our lives are in God's hands. Because God is sovereign, you know that the odds have nothing to do with the circumstances of your life. Yet you play the odds game in your head, even as you tell yourself that God—not fate—is in control.

How can we trust God when we've been dealt a death blow? It's not easy. I have found that it helps to keep going back to God, reading his Word, praying, waiting in his presence. When I do, he gives grace and peace to carry me through the pain. He'll do the same for you.

> *Trust in the LORD with all your heart*
> *and lean not on your own understanding;*
> *in all your ways acknowledge him,*
> *and he will make your paths straight.*

PROVERBS 3:5-6

"What If My Husband Didn't Believe in Jesus?"

No matter what a person's belief has been in life, we cannot know what happens between him and God in those very final moments before death. We are not to judge. All we can do is tell others the reason for the hope we have. An unbelieving husband may very well experience a change of heart and an encounter with the living God that remains unknown to us this side of heaven.

The biblical example that holds hope for our loved one is the story of the thief on the cross. Hanging there, close to death, this man said, "'Jesus, remember me when you come into your kingdom.' [And] Jesus answered him, 'I tell you the truth, today you will be with me in paradise'" (Luke 23:42-43). This private moment between Jesus and the man offers comfort when a loved one's faith is in question.

"Where Can I Find Comfort?"

LET YOURSELF CRY

Some days a good, hard cry brings healing to the soul. It is cleansing and wonderfully freeing.

When I needed to cry, my bathtub was my "dissolving spot." I'd wait till the girls were asleep, and then I'd retreat behind two doors and a hallway. I'd fill the tub with almost-scalding water, light candles, and put a tape of torch songs in the cassette player. As the melancholy music brought haunting memories of Jack and me in our younger days, I'd weep until I was spent. My soul ached with longing for what would never be again. My tears mixed with beads of sweat that drenched my face, soaking me with grief.

Then relief would come flooding in, overtaking the pain that had pierced me. I'd let my shoulders sink down into the water as I breathed in the comforting vapors of the steam and scented candles. God filled my heart with his peace.

God's comfort is mysterious and miraculous. It certainly can't be explained. How is it possible to be comforted when you've lost a loved one? God's touch transcends human reason. Somehow he comes and washes the open wounds of our soul with his love. Could it be he, too, knows how it feels to lose the one closest to you?

Find your own dissolving spot. Choose a private place where you won't be disturbed. Go there when you feel like crying and release all your emotions. Invite God to join you and to comfort you.

The LORD is close to the brokenhearted
and saves those who are crushed in spirit.

PSALM 34:18

COMFORT THROUGH A DREAM

Jack came to me one night in a dream. It was so real that I wouldn't even have thought it a dream, but I awoke and found myself in bed. Just that day I had said to someone, "I wish I could talk to Jack for five minutes, just five minutes. I just want to know if I am doing things the way he would want—things like the qualifications for the athletic award at the girls' school. I mean, it's named after him. I want it to reflect what he would want. Just five minutes."

My sympathetic listener sighed and said nothing. What was there to say? Jack would not be visiting me.

Then I dreamed he was there. I was in a car that had stopped along a deserted road. The door opened and Jack got in. He looked at me, smiled, and said, "I only have five minutes, but I just wanted to tell you that you are doing fine."

He sat and looked at me, never touching me, and I drank in the loving acceptance on his face. His hand opened the car door without his looking away from me. He stepped out of the car and closed the door. I woke up with tears streaming down my face. That was the only dream in which Jack gave me a message.

I don't believe we can communicate with the dead through mediums and séances. But God used dreams in the Old Testament to communicate with people, and I believe he can do that today if he chooses. Whether my dream was simply a dream, or more than that, I'll never know this side of heaven. But God used it to bring me hope and healing in the midst of great pain. He can do the same for you—through a dream or otherwise.

You Are on Dry Land

There were days when all kinds of disturbing thoughts swirled through my mind: *Will I ever be happy again? Will my children be forever scarred by their father's death? Will I make wise choices about finances? Will I be able to earn a living?*

On those days I had a hard time believing I would survive widowhood. I had to remind myself over and over again that my feelings were not an indication of the actual condition of my life. Intellectually I believed the promises of God, but at times I was still so afraid. I longed for peace, but sometimes I saw only a frightening future ahead.

Then a scripture came to mind that I wrote down on an index card and carried with me everywhere:

> Then Moses stretched out his hand over the sea, and all
> that night the LORD drove the sea back with a strong
> east wind and turned it into dry land. The waters were
> divided, and the Israelites went through the sea on dry

ground, with a wall of water on their right and on their left. (Exodus 14:21-22)

While crossing the Red Sea in their escape from Egypt, the children of Israel must have been terrified. Walls of water towered above them on both sides, and Pharaoh's army chased them from behind. But they walked on dry land. Not slippery mud or slowing slush. Dry land!

We, too, are on dry land. No matter what our emotions tell us, we have God's promise that we are on solid footing as long as we follow him.

"CAN OUR LOVED ONES SEE US?"

Many years after Jack's death, I was watching *Always,* a movie about loss. Holly Hunter plays Dorinda, the vivacious, young pilot whose love, Pete (played by Richard Dreyfuss), dies in a plane crash.

One particular scene touched me even though it had been years since my own loss. On a lazy, summer evening about a year after Pete's death, Dorinda slips a tape into a player and listens nostalgically to the song that she and Pete had dubbed their own. The melancholy strains of "Smoke Gets in Your Eyes" fill the room, and Dorinda begins to sway as if dancing with Pete.

Tears spilled down my cheeks as I once again experienced the physical ache of Jack's death. I watched Dorinda slow dance with her invisible partner and sobbed with the pain of absence. I missed so much about Jack! His touch. His clean-shaven cheek resting against my upturned face. His arm holding me close. His grace as a dance partner. The memories were at once wonderful and excruciating.

In the movie, the audience has an advantage over the partnerless Dorinda. We can see the ghostlike image of Pete who glides undetected around Dorinda's swaying body.

"I know you can't see me, but I can see you," Pete silently whispers.

Many widows have asked me, "Do you think our loved ones can see us?"

We certainly want them to. We imagine them present. I've had many moments when I am convinced that Jack must see what is happening in my life or in the lives of our children.

I cannot prove this theologically, but I know we are surrounded by spiritual realities that we can't see. And I also believe there are unexplainable moments when we can sense the presence of our departed loved ones.

However, living in a fantasy is unhealthy. It inhibits our ability to fully live today. So don't dally with strange spirits and illusions. Instead, allow yourself moments of mystery in the protection of God's care. If you sense the presence of a departed loved one, simply smile and be content with the realities you know.

> *No eye has seen, no ear has heard, no mind has con-*
> *ceived what God has prepared for those who love him.*

> 1 CORINTHIANS 2:9

YOUR HUSBAND IS SAVING YOU
A SEAT AT A BANQUET

Scripture tells us that heaven is like a wedding banquet (see Matthew 22). This particular image of heaven came to life for me one dreary, Sunday morning while I was visiting a beautiful, old stone church, designed like a European cathedral. At the front of the sanctuary a massive stained-glass window glimmered with scenes of Jesus and his disciples.

The pastor asked the congregation to look up at the window and envision it opening up and a large banquet table extending into the heavens. He went on to paint a picture of the celebration that we will be part of when we all are with the Lord. There will be no pain, no tears of sorrow. We will be at the same table with God himself, and we'll have an eternity of new life ahead of us. It was, and is, an exciting thought.

Then I saw a new heaven and a new earth, for the first heaven and the first earth had passed away, and there was no longer any sea. I saw the Holy City, the new Jerusalem, coming down out of heaven from God, prepared as a bride beautifully dressed for her husband. And I heard a loud voice from the throne saying, "Now the dwelling of God is with men, and he will live with them. They will be his people, and God himself will be with them and be their God. He will wipe every tear from their eyes. There will be no more death or mourning or crying or pain, for the old order of things has passed away." He who was seated on the throne said, "I am making everything new!" Then he said, "Write this down, for these words are trust-worthy and true."

REVELATION 21:1-5

NEW AND GLORIOUS BODIES

I remember picturing Jack in heaven when I was asked to choose the clothes I wanted him to be buried in. Now, I believe that his soul went immediately to heaven. And Scripture tells us that we will have new bodies in heaven, so I don't know why I even worried about what was covering his earthly body. But I picked out a traditional outfit of khaki slacks, a white shirt, navy and gold tie, navy blue blazer, socks and loafers. Picturing him alive in heaven, walking around in perfectly beautiful surroundings, I felt secure that my choice would please him. Then I realized that I had forgotten to include a belt. I felt terrible. Jack was a meticulous dresser and would never have walked around beltless.

Then I laughed at myself and my limited picture of heaven. Many aspects of heaven are shrouded behind a veil of mystery, but we are told that we will have new bodies—perfect, pain-free, and unravaged by earthly age. We'll be perfectly—gloriously!—dressed in heaven's most wondrous attire.

> *Our citizenship is in heaven. And we eagerly await*
> *a Savior from there, the Lord Jesus Christ, who, by*
> *the power that enables him to bring everything*
> *under his control, will transform our lowly bodies*
> *so that they will be like his glorious body.*
>
> PHILIPPIANS 3:20-21

OUR HUSBANDS SEE CLEARLY

We who are left behind are limited in our ability to understand God and his purposes. Our vision is blurred by this sin-tainted world. As soon as we gain one insight, another challenge pops up in front of us. But our husbands are no longer hindered by such obstructions. They are in the presence of God and enjoying the rewards of that close communion. Heaven is a place of transparency without fear—knowing and being known, accepting and being accepted, loving and being loved.

> *Now we see but a poor reflection as in a mirror;*
> *then we shall see face to face. Now I know in part;*
> *then I shall know fully, even as I am fully known.*
>
> 1 Corinthians 13:12

A PLACE OF LASTING JOY

I remember talking to my children about heaven and likening it to a long and fabulous vacation. But that description falls far short. Earthly vacations often have their share of challenges, including expense, possible illness, bad weather, missed connections, lost luggage, and always having to come back to the dailiness of life.

Not so with heaven. Perfect always and forever and ever—who can even imagine?!

My heart is glad and my tongue rejoices;
  my body also will rest secure,
because you will not abandon me to the grave,
  nor will you let your Holy One see decay.
You have made known to me the path of life;
  you will fill me with joy in your presence,
  with eternal pleasures at your right hand.

PSALM 16:9-11

A TASTE OF HEAVEN

For a number of years, Jack and I were involved in an international evangelism training program. Twice a year, pastors from all over the world gathered at Coral Ridge Presbyterian Church, Fort Lauderdale, Florida, and learned the techniques that we used year-round.

At one particular training seminar, after seven days of workshops and three nights of calling on people in the surrounding area, we ended the training with a session in the main sanctuary.

Many people had made professions of faith, and the excitement level was high.

The last thing we all did together was to form a large circle around the outside row of pews, join hands, and sing "We Are One in the Spirit." Many nations were represented. People of diverse backgrounds and cultures sang in stunning harmony. Tears of joy flowed freely down the faces of men and women; eyes were closed or looking heavenward; hands were joined and raised. It was a taste of what is to come.

> *After this I looked and there before me was a great*
> *multitude that no one could count, from every*
> *nation, tribe, people and language, standing before*
> *the throne and in front of the Lamb.*
>
> REVELATION 7:9

"Help! I Never Wanted to Be a Single Parent!"

"I'm Afraid to Discipline Too Much!"

"I'm afraid to discipline my children too much," Judy told me with tears in her eyes. "They've been through so much, I don't want to hurt them. But they are really out of hand." Children suffer the loss of a father in ways they often cannot articulate. Surging emotions pull them to and fro as their little minds and hearts absorb the impact of their loss. Because they don't have the vocabulary to express their feelings, children often voice their grief through disruptive behavior or disobedience.

And sometimes children are just being children; sometimes they push the limits to see how much they can get away with. Their behavior may be normal kid stuff and not intentionally aggressive.

When widowhood plunged me into single parenting, I dubbed myself a benevolent dictator, with the emphasis on *benevolent*. My young children didn't get to vote on many issues. They were not able to make choices that fell into the realm of adult decision-making.

Your children need you to be the chief decision-maker in your family. Kindness and firmness can go hand in hand. Never abdicate your role as parent. Children need guidance and help in learning to integrate their loss into their lives in a way that helps them grow, not to use it as an excuse for disruptive behavior.

If you are struggling in this area, talk with some parents you admire about how they lovingly discipline their children. Talk with your kids and assure them that you love them. Let them know that with God's help you are able to lead your household in an orderly and responsible fashion.

SHIELDING YOUR CHILD FROM MORE PAIN

I remember walking slowly back to the car where my little daughters stood crying after watching their father die in a fiery accident. They seemed rooted to the ground in fear as I pulled them close to me. "I don't know how," I whispered, "but I promise you that we will be okay." I was on my knees with one arm wrapped around each child. I tried to say comforting words and assure them that we would survive. But I told God in the silence of my heart, "I will never let these children suffer like this again." I said it not with anger but with deep conviction.

Of course I couldn't fulfill that vow. No one could. My daughters have been hurt many times since the death of their father. This has been particularly challenging because I so wanted—and still want—to protect them from enduring any more than they had already suffered.

If you have young children, love them and hug them. Pray that God's angels will surround them and carry them through all the painful moments of life.

> *When you pass through the waters,*
> *I will be with you;*
> *and when you pass through the rivers,*
> *they will not sweep over you.*
> *When you walk through the fire,*
> *you will not be burned;*
> *the flames will not set you ablaze.*

Isaiah 43:2

"That's Not How Daddy Used to Do It"

"Daddy wouldn't have done it that way!"

Those words ring in the ear of every widow who is a mother.

I used to feel guilty because I knew Jack would have done some things differently. I would try to remember things we'd talked about regarding the girls and second-guess what Jack would do if he were still alive.

Then I heard my married friends complaining of similar attempts by their children to play one parent against the other. I remembered my own ability to run between my parents to try to get my own way if one of them said no. I realized that even if Jack had lived, I would still have had to wrestle with how to do things.

Children who have lost their father can sculpt him into a perfect figure, posing him high on a golden pedestal, and they use that image to make mom feel inadequate. I finally stopped trying to live up to Jack's image and admitted the obvious: Daddy isn't here, no matter how perfect he might have been. "So, girls, you're stuck with me. What I say goes," I told them.

Let go of trying to live exactly as you would live if your husband were still alive.

Do the best you can to instill those important values that your husband wanted for your children, and trust your own ability to parent effectively on your own.

✑⁓

KIDS LONG TO BE "NORMAL"

Lisa had been without her father for almost eight years when she headed out to California as a college freshman. She and I packed up all her belongings and unpacked them in the dorm room that she was to share with three other girls. Two sets of bunk beds, four desks and four built-in dressers and closets were adorned with all the trappings of teenage girls on their first adventure away from home. Clothes, makeup, all manner of electronic gear, and pictures. The top shelf of Lisa's desk held about a dozen framed photographs that captured special moments of her life with her family, including some of her and Jack during the last years of his life.

A few months later, I made the first of many trips to see Lisa and spend the weekend with her. I rented a car at the airport, checked hastily into my hotel, and headed for her dorm. She was waiting for me as I knocked on the door of the suite her room was in. Her room looked well lived in. I smiled at the stacks of CDs and magazines and the portable makeup cases bulging with enough cosmetics to last a decade. I stopped by the shelf of pictures and lingered on those of Jack with Lisa. "Have you told your room-mates about Daddy?" I asked, knowing she would know what I meant.

"No," she replied with no further comment.

I was so surprised. In asking the question I had fully expected her to say yes.

"Why not?"

"I just want to feel normal," she answered quietly, with no invitation to continue this discussion. I let it go, but I thought a lot about what she had said.

Lisa felt different, and perhaps stigmatized, because she came from a single-parent family. I had felt that way as a single mom, but it hadn't occurred to me that my children might also feel awk-ward after almost eight years.

Later that weekend, I encouraged Lisa to tell her roommates that her father had died when she was ten years old. She nodded sadly, but I knew she would manage to get it out in her own timing.

All of us—even children—need to feel "normal." Talk with

your kids about how they feel about being part of a single-parent family. Encourage them to be open with trusted friends, but don't push them. Extroverted children may open up much sooner and more often than introverted children. Allow both types of personalities to adjust at their own pace.

You Have All You Need
to Be a Good Parent

In losing Jack, I lost the father of my children. My grief was compounded by theirs.

Jack and I met in high school. He was strong and self-confident, and I relied on him greatly. We made many decisions together, especially with regard to the children, but because he was very wise, I often agreed with him without hesitation. I missed his parenting insights deeply. I remember looking in the mirror and asking myself how in the world I could parent those little ones on my own.

As the days and weeks passed, I learned to cling to God's promise that he is "a father to the fatherless, a defender of widows"

(Psalm 68:5). God didn't speak to me in an audible voice or appear at the breakfast table with advice for the day. But a growing sense of self-confidence and God-reliance seeped into the parenting void that Jack used to fill.

I listened to the counsel of godly friends and read recommended articles and books. Mostly I sat with a written list in my hand before my Father and asked for his help. Over time God gave me the assurance that I could be a good mom. I hadn't felt that way even before Jack died. It felt good, freeing, to say, "I can do this."

You have all you need to be the parent God wants you to be. If you don't feel this now, bring your concerns to the Father. Talk to him, wait, cry, listen. Go about your day. Sit before him again with your questions. See what happens.

> *His divine power has given us everything we need*
> *for life and godliness through our knowledge of him*
> *who called us by his own glory and goodness.*
>
> 2 PETER 1:3

"Now you have to be both mother and father to your children."
The well-meaning people who said this to me were trying to offer
empathy and support, and at first I took their words to heart.

But I failed.

I wasn't Jack. He was big, strong, athletic, a night person who
would stay up late to play with the girls on Friday nights, a floor
wrestler, an impish kid-at-heart on the playground, a male presence in their lives.

I was not and never will be my children's father, and neither will
you be a father to your children. A load was lifted from my shoulders when I gave up this false expectation. I encourage you to do the
same.

While it's true that no one can replace their father, your children
still need men in their lives. Male family friends can sometimes
stand in the gap, taking your kids to ball games or on fishing
trips, teaching them how to change the oil in a car or how to
mow the lawn, giving them hugs and showing interest in them
personally. Teachers, coaches, pastors, youth workers, and your
own family members can provide male role models for your kids.

Concentrate on being the best mother you can be and foster
relationships with reliable and trustworthy family and friends—

and entrust your kids to the God who is "a father to the father-less" (Psalm 68:5).

IF YOUR CHILD IS AFRAID OF THE DARK

Many young children envision perilous dangers lurking in their closets and under their beds as soon as the bedroom lights are turned off at night. Children who have lost a father to death face these same fears, and unlike other children, they know that some-times their worst fears *do* come true.

Lisa never experienced this bedtime angst, but Lara did. I would read the Bible as I tucked Lara in under the covers. Then we'd pray and I'd talk with her about God and his angels protecting her. But no matter what our routine was, she was still afraid of the dark. I put a night-light in her room, but the light was too dim for comfort. Lara couldn't fall asleep unless the overhead light was on.

I talked and cajoled and tried to convince her to sleep with the light off. Nothing worked. Then one day I asked myself what was the big deal anyway. What was so damaging about just letting her sleep with the light on? I decided that relieving Lara's fear was far more important.

I left the light on, and she fell asleep peacefully. Later that evening I turned off the overhead light and switched on the night-light. Lara gradually began to use the night-light instead of the overhead light. She eventually became a sleeper who preferred no light at all.

Some of your children's fears will be difficult to relieve. Fear of the dark, however, is easily remedied. Your pediatrician or family doctor will also be able to give you suggestions on how to help your child sleep peacefully.

YOUR CHILD'S FEAR OF YOUR DEATH

Children who have lost their father are usually afraid they will also lose their mother. Even though this is normal, it can be very disturbing for children.

When Lara and Lisa began expressing their fear that I might die too, I decided to have them talk with a counselor. My older daughter, Lisa, resisted, consistent with her introverted nature, but I sent both of them anyway.

I spoke with the counselor first and told him about Jack's death and that the girls were afraid of losing me as well. He assured me that he would not gloss over the issue but would talk directly with them about what would happen to them if I did die. This sounded scary, but I knew it was for their best. The girls and I had already talked about the couple who would be their guardians if something happened to me. They loved this couple and knew they would be cared for and loved.

After the counseling session, Lisa and Lara said little about what had transpired. The counselor told me privately that they had talked openly and had listened carefully to him as he reviewed with them how well they would be cared for in the event of my death. Tough stuff. But such a discussion addressed their fear of abandonment. They still struggled, but both girls seemed less anxious and more able to let me out of their sight without extreme fear.

If you have kids, don't put off making arrangements for their care in the event of your own death. Be sure you have an updated will that covers all eventualities, including guardianship. Talk with your children about how loved and cared for they would be. Then don't dwell on fearful issues, but draw their attention to the present, to your love and commitment to them, and to their heavenly

Father's even greater love. If your children's fear is unrelieved by these discussions, don't hesitate to send them to a counselor.

Putting First Things First

"My friends keep encouraging me to have an active social life," Anne told me. She had been a widow for about a year. "They think I am neglecting myself and that I'll never meet any men who might be potential husbands. The trouble is, I am so tired and my kids seem to resent my being out too often at night."

I'd had similar conversations during the years when I spent almost every weekend night and several weeknights in gymnasiums watching my girls play volleyball and basketball. "You'll never get remarried if you are always with your kids," lamented one assertive matchmaker.

Well-meaning people sometimes put pressure on widows to be socially active and eventually remarry. They believe that remarriage is the goal of every widowed woman. Most widows I know do want to remarry someday, but putting your social life ahead of your children's needs is a mistake.

When my children were still in elementary school, a Friday or Saturday social event didn't interfere with their schedule. But as soon as Lisa entered junior high, all that changed. She became involved in sports, and our evenings filled up with one event after another. A few years later, Lara began a similar routine. Between practices, games, and tournaments, I had little time for other activities.

And I loved it. I decided to be at *all* their games: home and away games, weeknights and weekend nights. Once the decision was made, it was easy. Not everyone understood my commitment, and some frowned at my seemingly unbalanced life. One man invited me to a Christmas party that happened to be on the same night as one of the girl's basketball games. When I declined his invitation, he was aghast that I would choose to miss a once-a-year party for a game that was played several times a week.

I am not suggesting that you make the same sweeping decision as I did. I enjoy sports and wouldn't have wanted to be elsewhere. You may not feel the same and making such a commitment would be more of a sacrifice. You might decide to have one night out a week for yourself or to devote certain evenings to be with your children and leave other nights open for negotiation. Whatever you decide, I am recommending that you communicate to your children that they come before your social life, and then stick to that decision.

The investment you make in the lives of your children will be worth the effort. Kids need both quality time *and* quantity time. You also need time with other adults and entertainment that refreshes you, but strive for a balance that gives your children the comfort and assurance that they are your first priority.

"I Can't Remember What Daddy Looked Like"

By the time Lara was a junior in high school, her father had been gone for nine years. She spoke of him often and adorned her room with pictures of them together.

During one particular week that year, I noticed that she was sitting on her bed every night, slowly leafing through the pages of a photo album and crying softly. The album was one that I had made for each of the girls. Many of the pictures were eight-by-ten-inch school photos of Jack from high school and college. The pages bulged with action shots and newspaper clippings. I didn't interrupt Lara, knowing she was just remembering her dad and feeling sad that he wasn't alive to see her play basketball.

After a week of the same scenario each night, I went in and sat on the edge of her bed.

"What are you doing honey?" I asked softly.

Looking up through tears she said, "I can't remember what Daddy looks like. Every night I stare at these pictures and try to remember, but then I just can't."

I hugged her, and we cried together. Then I took the album and gently closed it. "You don't have to remember," I told her. "You will be with Daddy again. For now, enjoy the pictures and the memories that you do have, and stop worrying about seeing him in your mind. Daddy will always live in your heart, and he is alive right now in heaven."

She smiled and wiped her tears.

Once-clear memories eventually fade from our minds and our children's minds, and we need not struggle to hang on to them. Assure your children that a dimmed memory is not a disloyalty. Even though their memories have faded, their love for their dad will live in their hearts forever.

Remembering As the Years Go By

You and your children will always remember the anniversary of your husband's death. While this is not an anniversary to be celebrated, it is important to acknowledge your loss.

My daughters and I never established a ritual that we repeated every year. Sometimes we did something together that their dad would have enjoyed; sometimes we had a special meal together after school; sometimes we exchanged notes and a few spoken words.

When we became separated geographically, I started to remember the day in a simple way that I have continued, even though we now live close together again. I send each of my girls a dozen roses every December 15 with a card that says, "Remembering. Love, Mom."

As the years pass, your way of remembering the anniversary of your husband's death will change and evolve. Do whatever seems most meaningful and comforting for you and your children. Sometimes less is more, and your children will prefer to experience this day without much outward expression. It doesn't mean they don't remember or feel deeply.

LOSING YOUR HUSBAND WHEN YOUR CHILDREN ARE GROWN

Nina was in her early fifties when her husband died. Her three children were grown and living away from her home. "They were a tremendous support when Ron died," she said. "But now they have trouble treating me like an adult. They're hovering and constantly checking up on me. I appreciate their concern, but I am a big girl."

Nina's sentiments echo those of many widows with adult children. They love and appreciate their children and their concern, but they struggle with developing a balance in their relationship that allows them to retain their independence while allowing their children to offer comfort and support.

Not all women are like Nina. Some respond in an opposite way, becoming more and more dependent on their adult children. If they begin to rely too heavily on their children, this can strain the relationship.

If your children are adults, give them time to adjust to the loss of their father and the implications of that on their relationship with you. Allow them time and space to help you. But if their enthusiasm becomes intrusive, gently and lovingly talk with them about the ways you would like for them to engage with you. Schedule times to have them over or to go out with them. Communicate with them about ways you are managing well and are feeling good about yourself for being able to handle new things. Thank them for their concern and offers of help, but be specific about what you want to take care of on your own and what you would appreciate help on.

But if you are relying on your kids to take care of nearly all of your needs—asking them to accompany you or to drive you to appointments when you can drive yourself, calling them and crying on the phone after the first few weeks, planning most of your social events with them instead of with friends your age—you will need to become more responsible for yourself. If you know you are doing this or are unsure whether you are, talk with your children and ask them to be honest with you. Don't get angry or defensive if they express frustration with your reliance on them. Take that information and use it to make changes. Cultivate friendships, join groups at your church, go to a grief workshop, talk with existing friends. You will feel much better for it.

If your adult children are not helpful, grieve that loss and initiate interaction with them. If they still don't respond, back off and entrust them to God. Usually, adult children respond to you in much the same way they always have. If you were distant from them before your husband's death, that distance may remain afterward.

THE WIDOW WITHOUT CHILDREN

If you and your husband had hoped to have children, your loss will be compounded by the death of this dream. The childless widows I've met who wanted children express a deep sadness that they don't have the physical extension of their husband living on in his children. They are missing what never came to be and will never be in the future. They may remarry and have children, but they will not see the imprint of their first husband on any of those little ones.

Give yourself time to grieve for what did not happen. Go before God and cry out your pain to him. Ask him to heal this aspect of your journey through widowhood just as you ask him to heal all other painful portions of your heart.

"WHO PROVIDES THE SPIRITUAL DIRECTION FOR MY CHILDREN?"

I was speaking about single parenting at a conference on the East Coast a few years ago. One of my points was that children in single-mother homes need spiritual direction, and the mother is primarily responsible for that teaching.

A hand shot up from the back of the room, and a man called out to get my attention. He stood up and began to tell me that I was not speaking scripturally. He said that it was the responsibility of the church to provide male leadership for single women and their children. I asked him if his church provided such a service, and he murmured, "No," and quickly sat down.

God says that he is the father to the fatherless and the defender of widows, and that there is one mediator between man and God, Jesus Christ. Single mothers who know Jesus personally have direct access to him, his guidance, and his help.

Your church may teach male leadership in the home, but know that as a single mom you have the responsibility and the spiritual resources to be that leader in the absence of your husband. You are now responsible for teaching your children spiritual truths. Trust God to give you wisdom and insight as you seek to mold and shape your children's hearts toward him.

Perhaps you married when you were past the age of having children, or maybe you and your husband chose not to have children. You are not grieving a loss that did not occur, but you are grieving the loss of your spouse without the comfort that children bring. You may not have family calling to check on you or invite you to join them for social times.

It's important not to succumb to isolation. Maintain friendships or, if friends seem few and far between, try to cultivate new ones. This can be done in the context of grieving if you join a grief workshop or widows' group. Couples are healthy companions too. Don't cut yourself off. Be around others. It will help you heal.

> *A father to the fatherless, a defender of widows, is*
> *God in his holy dwelling.*
>
> PSALM 68:5

"How Do I Deal with Other People?"

SOAK IN THE LOVE

In the weeks after Jack's death, friends and family stepped in and took over many of my daily tasks. People took turns cleaning the house and cooking all our meals. A friend picked up our laundry and returned it, clean and neatly folded. A man from our church came every week and cut the grass. These acts of love allowed me time to get through the difficult days of adjustment and added responsibility.

I called a friend from the scene of Jack's accident, and she was at our house by the time I got home. She handled the continuous phone calls. That evening I asked her to stay with the girls and me for the first few weeks, just to help me get through the days. As we talked for hours on end, she became my lifeline. The weeks turned into a month, and I asked my friend to stay on indefinitely. She agreed. This dear friend lived with us for two years. During that time, I was on the receiving end of a friendship that has lasted and grown to this day.

In the early days of your loss, graciously accept help. When healing has strengthened you, you will begin to give again. For now, soak in the love others want to shower on you and your family.

When Everyone Has an Opinion

My mother was appalled that I never put flowers on Jack's grave. She thought it was disrespectful, and she worried that other people would think I didn't miss him. I explained to her that I didn't think of Jack as being in that grave, and that he would have wanted me to spend that money for something other than graveside flowers.

My mother died almost nine years ago, and every Christmas and Easter I order a large floral arrangement for her grave. Does that seem inconsistent? I want to respect both my husband and my mother in a manner that they would have wished. I care much more about what mattered to those two people I loved very much than about what other people may think about my actions.

You will have to make myriad choices: legal, financial, business, personal, spiritual, and parental, from the buying and selling of property to the accessories you want on your next car. Some of these decisions will come easily, and you will feel confident about your choices. Others will cause sleepless nights and anxious nail biting.

In the days ahead, you will receive all kinds of advice—some good, some bad. Pray for discernment and seek godly counsel. In small issues, learn to make the decisions and then relax. In big issues, draw on the wisdom of others whom you can trust. Talk to God about what choices to make.

"No One Mentions His Name"

For a few weeks after Jack's memorial service, my friends and I talked of nothing else but him. We laughed and cried and looked at pictures. Our reminiscing helped ease the pain caused by the wrenching away of a life so entwined with ours.

Then, with the exception of a few people, people stopped talking about Jack. There was an unspoken decision to move on. I felt as if everyone had simply buried the memory with the man. Others had told me this would happen, but I still wasn't prepared. I wanted to keep talking because talking meant remembering. I wanted to say Jack's name out loud, over and over. *Jack, Jack, Jack!* Saying his name helped me remember all that he was to me, and it hurt me that others seemed uncomfortable talking about him.

I know now that silence from others doesn't mean callousness or lack of feeling. It is one of the ways that people deal with grief. Eventually I grew more comfortable with other's discomfort about mentioning even the name of my husband around me. You will too.

"WHY DON'T YOU CRY?"

I was walking into church one Sunday morning when a woman came up to me, grabbed me by the shoulders, and shook me. "Why don't you cry?" she demanded. I was so startled I didn't say a word. She let go of me and walked off in exasperation. *Wow*, I thought to myself, *she's really upset with me.*

People express grief in deeply personal ways. Some weep openly and often. Others, like me, don't reveal their deepest feelings much in public.

All of us look at others and draw conclusions from their actions or lack of action; we assume, conclude, judge. It's helpful to realize other people do the same to us. I don't think their motives are any more suspect than mine are. They don't mean to be hurtful. In fact, much of the time their conclusions reflect where they are rather than where they think we are.

Forgive those who unintentionally hurt you by evaluating your grief and telling you how you should be responding. Forgive them and then grieve in your own way.

Soul Friends

In those early days of grief—and the days since—three women faithfully and unconditionally accepted and supported me. Many others touched and comforted me in a multitude of ways, but those three are soul friends.

Soul friends know all about you and love you anyway. They have the patience to walk with you through dark times, times when it would be easier to leave you to your own misery. Soul friends are with you for the long haul. They are burden bearers. These saints are at your side in a hospital, at a grave, and on many a lonely night in the years after you're widowed.

These supporters make a huge difference in the lives of widows, and they pay a heavy price. They give of their time, their emotion, their energy. They experience personal pain on your behalf. Thank God for them. Remember them. As you grow stronger, let them know how grateful you are for them.

FEWER CLOSE RELATIONSHIPS

Any schedule I had maintained before Jack's death was nowhere to be found afterward. My life was turned upside down. He wasn't there to drive the kids to school or to pick up bread on the way home from the office. He wasn't there to fix the stopped-up toilet or to mow the lawn. He wasn't there to balance our checkbook or to pay the monthly bills.

All the details of our lives now fell to me. The added responsibilities consumed my time and energy. I didn't anticipate how this would impact my friendships, but it resulted in the slow and unintentional end to some. I had little regular contact with many women I had previously seen often. And because I was single, I wasn't invited to as many social events by some couples Jack and I had known in the past.

It is still sometimes painful for me to look at old pictures and see people with whom I was once close. They were an important part of my life. But my priorities changed, and I had to let go.

You may need to do the same. You may feel exhausted, unable to keep up some of your former contacts. Do what you can and graciously let go of those relationships that begin to dwindle. Some people will be in your life no matter what, and others will fade. People move in and out of our lives, but God stays forever.

And surely I am with you always, to the very end of the age.

MATTHEW 28:20

Recognizing Other People's Pain

On December 15, 1998, nineteen years after Jack's death, I picked up the phone to hear a young man's voice. It was Jimmy (he now goes by James, but he'll always be Jimmy to me), the son of dear friends—one of those couples who are in our lives forever. When Jimmy was in high school, he was close to Jack. Jack and I traveled around south Florida and enthusiastically cheered Jimmy on in his basketball successes. Our families were often at each other's homes and enjoyed many rich times together.

When Jack died, Jimmy was away at college. He came home for the memorial service and was obviously upset and shocked by this sudden loss. Just two days after Jack's accident, Jimmy received a letter from Jack. It had been written and mailed the day before the accident. It was just a note to say hi, and to encourage Jimmy in his current pursuits. That letter is now framed and has hung on a wall of Jimmy's home ever since.

I am often in touch with Jimmy's parents, but have spoken with him less frequently as the years have passed. So I was surprised to hear his voice on the phone last December.

"Hi, Lois," he said tentatively.

"Hi, Jimmy!"

"I just called…," he stammered. He couldn't finish and was choking back audible sobs. Jimmy hung up, and I sat in stunned silence. The depth of his pain so many years later moved me deeply.

A few minutes later the phone rang again, and Jimmy's mother was on the line. Jimmy had called her to explain what he had tried to do but couldn't quite complete. He had asked her to call me and explain because he didn't think he could get out the words to me personally.

Of course, I knew. He had called to tell me he remembered. He remembered Jack and that day so long ago, and that December 15 marked another anniversary. Marian and I talked and cried a little and shared the bittersweet communion of those who have suffered a common loss.

When we lose a spouse, we and our children receive most of the comfort and concern. But others suffer, too. Remember their pain and pray God will comfort them as well.

PART II

WHEN YOU'RE
READY TO
MOVE AHEAD

"How Do I Move on with My Life?"

Putting Away the Photos

One day, several years after Jack's death, I looked around and saw my home in a new light. Jack's photographs seemed oddly out of place. I realized that I pictured him having a wonderful time in heaven much more than I thought about him as he was captured in the photos.

At first the thought of removing those photographs seemed disloyal. Would people think that I had forgotten him? That I didn't want to be reminded of him? Those voices nagged me for a few days. Then I decided to talk with Lisa and Lara and tell them why I was going to change many of the photos: It was time to focus on our lives in the present and the future.

They understood, and we lovingly stored the visual account of their dad's life.

Cleaning Out the Closet

One of the most painful tasks a widow performs is removing her husband's personal belongings from their bedroom: his clothes from the closet and dresser, the clutter of items he kept on the bureau, the stack of magazines next to his side of the bed. It's as if each item carries the traces of conversations and imprints of moments you experienced together, including your most intimate moments.

Many widows put off this task for months. But the day will come when you will be ready to let go and make the bedroom your own. When is up to you. It took me many months.

There's a cowboy in Davie, Florida (yes, Florida does have cowboys!), wearing a T-shirt with my picture on it, a photographic image imprinted on a yellow shirt that Jack had proudly worn when cutting the grass or shooting hoops in the driveway. That shirt was swept into one of the boxes that contained most of Jack's clothes. I had left his side of our closet untouched for many months after his death. I couldn't face another empty half. I already had so many: his side of the car, his side of the bed, his chair at the table, his end of the couch, his place in the pew, his voice on the other end of the phone, his active presence in all parts of my heart.

So I avoided removing his clothes from his side of our walk-in closet. Then one day in May, I asked a friend to come over and help me take away the most personal of his belongings. I buried my face in his shirts and inhaled deeply. His scent still lingered, evoking sweet memories. Grief welled up inside me, and tears flowed, releasing pain from somewhere deep inside.

My friend and I sorted through each memory-laden item, saving a few basketball jerseys, an army flight jacket, and his graduation cap and gown. I stacked his T-shirts without looking at each one. Later I realized, with a smile, that the one with my photo was among the bunch.

I watched out the window as my friend's car headed off to Davie to donate the clothing to a charity. Then I sat in the closet and cried.

Whether with a friend, a family member, or alone, clean out the closet. Choose your own time, but face the pain.

I became a widow at thirty-four. I was young and dependent and naive about the world, although I didn't think so at the time. In our marriage I had seldom expressed a contrary opinion and was content to follow Jack's lead.

Then he was gone. Aspects of my personality began to emerge, aspects I hadn't known were there. I could be assertive when I needed to be; I could disagree graciously but firmly; I could make decisions that I'd never made before. It felt good.

Undoubtedly some of those changes would have come whether I had been widowed or not. But widowhood forces rapid change. And change brings with it a need to grieve and to rejoice— to grieve the loss of the old you and to rejoice at the birth of the new you.

Don't insist on remaining the same person you were. Recognize that even if your husband had lived, your perspectives and preferences would change. Allow yourself to become excited about how God will change and refine you. He can bring you joy that you never thought possible.

One of my good friends was widowed before I knew her. She is a spunky, outspoken, vivacious woman. She writes and speaks and travels and amazes her children and friends at the woman she has become. I am told that before her husband died, she was the same sweet person she is today, but she was painfully shy and retiring. She lived in her outgoing husband's shadow, and many expected that she would shrivel up and withdraw from life when he died.

She certainly didn't withdraw. She grew and changed and lives life fully.

You can too.

Taking Risks

Jack and I had lived in Florida for almost ten years when he was killed. I had intended to stay there for the rest of my life. But as the girls and I adjusted to life without him, we grew restless. While I knew it wasn't good to make big decisions during the first year of widowhood, by the time three years had passed, we began to consider a move across the country.

I visited a friend who lived in Colorado Springs, Colorado. Some of my friends thought I had lost my mind to even consider moving there. But for us it seemed right. I prayed and waited and talked with others for input. After a thoughtful process, I decided to take the risk and move.

It was a wonderful adventure for the girls and me, and it began a new phase of our lives. Not all risks are as dramatic as moving across country, but it is fun and exciting to begin to ask God to show you where he wants you to spread your wings.

BECOMING WONDER WOMAN

When the girls and I moved from Fort Lauderdale to Colorado Springs, we acquired a new family member: Heidi, a Siberian husky whose wintry look and wild spirit fit our new home. One morning I got up before Lisa and Lara and went downstairs to make my daily pot of coffee. I let Heidi outside and watched her run back and forth on our deck, sniffing the cool air and surveying her domain. I busied myself with the coffee making and wandered leisurely into the family room with my first steaming cup of the day.

Heidi was standing outside the back door with her face close to the doorknob. I automatically went over and let her in. She jaunted proudly past me, then turned around to display the bird that was crunched between her teeth.

I started screaming and pushed her outside. Her eyes, one blue and one brown, looked perplexed as she bit down on her prize. I stood watching and screaming as she swallowed every last feather of her captured prisoner.

"Oh no!" I cried out, wondering what awful disease she might get from eating a wild bird. I ran to the phone and called our veterinarian, only to get a recorded message of who to call for an emergency. Since it was certainly an emergency to me, I called the number and explained my dilemma. The woman who answered told me to pour hydrogen peroxide down Heidi's throat to induce vomiting.

I ran upstairs and rifled through the medicine closet, relieved to find an old bottle of hydrogen peroxide. I grabbed it and ran back downstairs. Reluctantly, I let Heidi inside and approached her. She wagged her tail and pranced a little, anticipating some playtime. I tried to grab her, but she liked our game of catch-me-if-you-can and managed to avoid my clutches. "Lisa!" I yelled. "Lisa! Get down here. Hurry, I need you," I continued to yell. Lisa came running, as she struggled to open her eyes. "Heidi ate a bird," I told her in rushed tones. "We have to get this hydrogen peroxide down her throat. Help me grab her and get her mouth open."

Lisa sprang into action, and we soon had our unsuspecting

prey in hand. I poured the liquid down her throat, and we pushed her out the door. Just as Lisa and I heaved sighs of relief, Heidi threw up the bird parts, but then she began to eat them again! With the verse about dogs returning to their vomit flitting through my mind, I ran outside and tried to shoo her away from her disgusting treasure. She finally retreated. I got a bucket of hot water and a broom and swept the morning's remains off the deck. By that time, I was in tears. "No one should have to do this," I said out loud.

But I did have to do it—and somehow I survived.

When I tell this story now, I can laugh about it. But it was not funny at the time. In the days ahead, you will find that you are able to do far more than you ever dreamed.

LEAVING ON A JET PLANE

"I never traveled before, but now I am on the go all the time!" Sybil said. In her late sixties when her husband died, Sybil had never been anywhere without him. Every year for over forty years they had taken a short summer vacation to the same beach resort.

Now Sybil has discovered the world of travel. She met her traveling buddies at a church group for widows. A few of the women who were seasoned travelers suggested they all take a trip together. Everyone had a ball. Between trips they enjoy getting together, taking classes, and supporting each other when difficulties strike.

When we lose a mate, we lose a lifestyle. We no longer have a ready companion for vacations or Friday nights; we experience a void that is difficult to fill. Even though you will never fill that hole in exactly the same way, you can branch out and develop new friendships and new endeavors. Female friendships can enrich your life by encouraging you to change and grow.

MOVING BEYOND LABELS

A friend came with me to a ladies' Bible study where I was to speak on singleness. After we introduced ourselves, we enjoyed easy small talk and delicious food for about a half-hour. Then we moved to the living room and pulled the chairs into a circle. The leader, who was the only married woman in the group, called us to order and opened with prayer. Then she asked us to go around the circle and say our names and "status."

My friend and I glanced at each other, and I asked the leader what she meant by "status."

She said, "Oh, you know, are you widowed, divorced, or never-married." I felt a shiver run up my spine and avoided making eye contact with my friend. Each woman said her name and then added the appropriate label in a resigned tone. I felt sad. The life of the single adult is often alien and isolated, and labels such as "divorced," "widowed," or "never-married" often intensify these feelings.

People are not defined by their marital status. It is simply one of the many facts about a person. Move beyond such labels and recognize the unique and significant place you occupy in the kingdom and in the heart of God.

CELEBRATE HOLIDAYS IN NEW WAYS

Our first Christmas without Jack was just ten days after his accident. I decided to cook dinner at home and have my parents over. This was how we had always celebrated Christmas, so we did it again. The next Christmas was similar, a mix of joy and sadness. Memories of happier days brought tears, blurring our vision all day long.

The third year we broke our pattern and had one of the best holidays ever. A close friend was living and working in Amsterdam at the time and had invited us to come over. At first I said no because I couldn't imagine not being home for Christmas. Then the more I thought about it, the more I liked the idea of celebrating in a new way.

Since our trip was our gift to each other, the girls and I boarded our plane bound for Amsterdam with no wrapped presents. Our hearts were light, and we were excited to soon see our friend. For the next two weeks, we traveled by train throughout Germany and Austria. It was cold and snowy, and we loved it. On Christmas Eve day, we all agreed to buy one small gift for each other to put under our three-foot tree that was lighted with real candles. It was a simple and enchanting Christmas.

Christmas isn't the only holiday that will be difficult, especially during the first year of loss. All holidays can be painful. There are birthdays, anniversaries, Mother's Day and Father's Day, and other days that are special to your family. One woman I know finds Memorial Day, the Fourth of July, and Labor Day difficult because her husband loved to host large barbecues on those days. To have parties on those holidays painfully reminds her of his absence, so now she takes her children away on those weekends or accepts invitations from friends to go to their homes.

Keep those traditions you feel comfortable with, and begin new ones that will enhance your life.

"What About *Men?*"

WHISPERED QUESTIONS

I have met with many widows over a cup of coffee. Almost always I'm asked about dating. Many widows fear that they are feeling things they should not feel. They worry that they would be scorned if anyone really knew what they were thinking. And so they risk asking one who has been where they now sit.

Here's what they want to know:

Should I feel guilty for having sexual desires?
No, sexual desires are normal.

I think a lot about a married man I know. What should I do?
Recognize your loneliness and vulnerability and the naturalness of your attachment to him. Don't be alone with him. Make a deliberate decision to turn your thoughts to something else when he comes into your mind. Accept that this temptation may be a

struggle, but make no moves in his direction and don't tell him you are attracted to him.

Some of my married women friends act strange when I am around. What is going on?

They may feel insecure and threatened by your presence around their husbands. Try to focus on them and don't, in any way, flirt with their husbands. Their strangeness may be due to their own insecurity and have little to do with you, but be sure your actions don't feed their fears.

A male married friend (pastor, leader at church, counselor) frequently calls me late in the evening and talks for a long time. Is this okay?

If his conversations with you are a secret, this is a red flag. Protect yourself and end the phone calls. If you don't answer his calls—get caller ID on your phone—he should get the message.

Some of these suggestions may sound overly cautious, but the number of widows who become involved in inappropriate ways is greater than many people think. While I am not aware of any statistics to support this statement, I can say that I am continually surprised at the number of women who tell me their stories when I am speaking at conferences. Just when I think I am with a group where this wouldn't be true, woman after woman comes to privately ask about her relationship with a married man.

Having said all of that, let me also say that if you set clear limits and boundaries for your relationships with men, you can enjoy wonderful friendships with married friends and single men.

When You Are Content to Stay Single

Remarriage is far from the mind of most new widows, but as time passes and healing comes, the idea of another partner often comes alive. But not always. Some women are genuinely content to remain single. They experience wholeness and fullness of life as single women and feel no desire or need to have a man in their lives. If you are one of these women, relax in your choice and fend off your well-meaning friends who try to be matchmakers.

It is often difficult for other people to understand why someone would want to remain alone, but your contentment might win them over in time.

Admitting Desire

Do you want to get married again? If so, you're not being disloyal to your husband by admitting it, so don't feel guilty.

Like most widows, I thought I would never want to remarry. But two years after Jack's death, I admitted to myself that I would like to get married again. I was never a loner, and I missed the companionship of one special man in my life. And I've always been a romantic. I longed to be part of a couple. I wanted to go through life with someone else and experience the intimacy that a spouse offers.

When I speak at singles' conferences, women often voluntarily tell me—repeatedly and loudly—that they don't want to date or remarry. But their behavior sends a different message. Such emphatic protestation usually is an attempt to deny a desire that we are afraid to face. Women who are truly content to be single typically don't broadcast that fact. They are busy living their lives and are not defensive about their singleness.

Being single or being married are equally acceptable choices. But you need to be honest with yourself and others about your true feelings—it's essential for navigating the rough waters of male-female relationships.

VULNERABILITY CAN LEAD
TO POOR CHOICES

When I was single, people used to tell me, "You are in a vulnerable position when it comes to relating to men."

"I know," I would reply.

But I didn't. Oh, I theoretically understood that loneliness influenced my thinking, but I never thought I would be tempted to become involved with men in any ungodly or unwise way. Then the months of singleness dragged into years, and my loneliness intensified. I found myself surrounded by married men, with few single men in sight. I began to accept the conclusion that statistics support: The odds of my remarrying were decreasing with every passing year.

Temptation simmered around and within the community of believers. I recognized my own undeclared emotional attachments to some of the married men around me, and I was stunned to admit that the ground on which I stood was more shaky than I had ever imagined.

Our culture's acceptance of morally compromising relationships has seeped through the walls of the church. Believers are buying the lie that we can follow Christ and at the same time be involved in affairs of the heart that do not honor God.

So be careful—careful of your feelings and rationalizations, of the compromises of others, of the influence of the culture, of your loneliness. We live in a world that provides loopholes for justifying all kinds of ungodly thinking and behavior, even inside the Christian community.

The Pain of Compromise

After the publication of my first book, *The Snare: Understanding Emotional and Sexual Entanglements,* I began to receive anonymous telephone calls from readers asking for help. Usually the callers were single women who had become involved with married men. These women, well beyond early temptations, were in deep pain when they called for help.

I listened to many stories of unintended compromise. While the names and specifics changed, the plot remained the same: pain of loneliness, kindness from a married man, seemingly innocent involvement, first physical involvement, relief from pain and continuance of contact, onset of guilt, and return of even greater pain than originally experienced.

Loneliness can drive us to make choices we never thought we would make. Involvement with an unavailable man is always the wrong solution, and it leads to pain compounded by guilt. With the help of the Holy Spirit and others who are committed to the same thing, choose to live by obedience. Grieve for those who stop struggling and give in to temptation. You *can* live as God desires. Keep in mind that supernatural resources are at your disposal.

Flee from sexual immorality. All other sins a man commits are outside his body, but he who sins sexually sins against his own body.

1 CORINTHIANS 6:18

Avoid Romanticizing Love and Dating

As a teenager I loved to pull a big, overstuffed chair up to the television and watch late-night movies. The black-and-white images leaped to life for me most Friday or Saturday nights after coming home from high-school games or gatherings. Handsome leading men wooed beautiful damsels with flattery and passionate kisses. The qualities of fidelity, commitment, and undying love drenched me with a romanticized view of love and relationships that I took with me into the world of adult dating.

I remember getting ready for my first date as a thirty-six-year-old single adult. I felt much the same as I had at age sixteen. I spent several hours primping, beginning with a long, steamy bubble bath. I dreamily pictured the upcoming evening as I soaked amid the bubbles. I just knew this first date would be a wonderful, romantic moment that would lead to other wonderfully romantic moments. But it wasn't romantic; it was far from my expectations, and I was disappointed.

When you finally feel ready to date, be realistic about what lies ahead. Adult dating is a minefield of explosives that can throw the most pragmatic woman off her feet. Balance your excitement and anticipation with a wariness about this unfamiliar terrain.

Be aware that most adults, yourself included, have a lot of baggage when they start dating again. When you meet someone, don't make decisions too quickly, either positively or negatively. Remember, it takes time to get to know someone and to understand the implications of their past on their present. While love at first sight may sound enticing, it can be risky. Proceed with caution.

⁂

The Rules Have Changed

As a married woman, you lived with few sexual restraints beyond monogamy. Now you find yourself single again, and you are once again called to celibacy. But the rules of dating have most likely changed during the years you were married. If you are naive, you may be caught unawares and make choices you later regret. Powerful emotions that were only emerging in youth or were freely expressed in marriage can seize the most rational woman and move her into a temptation with consequences far beyond those she has confronted before. Your firm convictions about sexual morality may waiver in the seductive breeze of passion.

Be wise and wary. Adult dating is far different from teenage dating. Years of marriage removed you from the need to restrict expression of your sexual feelings. Make a decision about your level of physical involvement—and stick to it.

LET GO OF COMPARISONS

When I started dating again, I couldn't help but compare every man with Jack. I had known him since high school and had been married to him for over thirteen years. One day I said to a friend, "Everyone seems so short. Where are all the tall men?"

Jack was six-foot-two, muscular, athletic, outgoing, and had blue eyes and black, curly hair. Everything about him—his looks, personality, profession, personal tastes—was well known to me. When I met someone new, I would think about Jack. No one compared well. I once heard it said that it is impossible to compete with the dead. It's true. A late husband is a tough act to follow.

Then as time went by, I found that I could care about men who were not at all like Jack. It became a matter of comparing apples and oranges and deciding both are fine. I chose to see each man I dated for who he was and not how he compared to Jack.

I encourage you to do the same. Let go of comparisons. Meet new men with a clean slate. Be open to who God made them to be. If you stop comparing, you will be able to view men for who they are while still appreciating who your late husband was.

BLIND DATES

One weekend a friend of mine asked me to entertain a couple visiting from Europe. I met these delightful people, and we enjoyed the sights of the West while becoming acquainted with each other. Over many conversations, I mentioned the blind dates I had endured. I never once thought about our cultural differences and just rambled on about the different men my friends had introduced me to. At the end of the day, the gentleman cautiously asked, "Why do you always go out with men who are blind?" We all had a good laugh as I explained what a blind date is.

Single women often complain about friends who seem intent

on trying to get them married off. But let's be honest about this: It is difficult to meet available men without the assistance of others. So if you do want to start dating again, let some trusted friends know, and be open to the risk of going on some blind dates.

Here are a few practical tips:

- Meet your date at a neutral, public location in the daytime.
- Drive your own car.
- Meet for coffee or for a designated short amount of time.
- Graciously decline another date if you don't care to meet him again.
- If you would like to see him again and he asks to see you, decide whether you want to have him come to your home.
- If you still have children at home, meet him away from your home until you know if this will be a more lasting relationship.
- If you are absolutely crazy about the man, move slowly.
- Remember that it takes time to get to know who someone really is.

Dating relationships are complex under the best of circumstances. It is wonderful to feel alive again. Your emotions zing all over the place, and your reason may take an extended vacation. New relationships may be part of God's plan for you, but there are lots of pitfalls. Be careful, prayerful, and accountable to trusted and wise friends.

THE PROBLEM OF PERCEPTIONS

"He's the most wonderful man you will ever meet," well-meaning friends often told me. But when I met this "wonderful man," I frequently found that my friends had perceived him through a glass darkly. No doubt they viewed me with equally blurred vision. Unfortunately, the result meant I spent time with men who were not a good match for me.

Jeannie told me, "My most shocking blind date was with a friend of friends of mine from church. They listed all the usual qualifications, and ended with the fact that this man was about forty-five. I was only twenty-eight at the time, but they were so eager that I agreed to meet him. I insisted on driving my own car and meeting them for lunch instead of meeting him alone for dinner. We set up a time and place.

"It was a beautiful day in southern California as I pulled into the restaurant parking lot. Spotting my friends' car, I parked next to them and got out. I couldn't believe my eyes when my friends and a man well into his fifties approached me. They excitedly introduced us, and I silently sighed at the prospect of an afternoon with a man old enough to be my father. I have no set rules about a particular age, but this man was thirty years older than I was, and I wasn't told the truth about his age. It was very disappointing."

Many of your friends would love to be the ones who find the perfect match for you. However, their enthusiasm may cloud their vision. Before agreeing to a blind date, ask a lot of questions and trust your gut reaction.

❦

IF MR. RIGHT DOES COME ALONG

Just when it seems impossible, there he is.

I had been single for almost ten years before I remarried. I had all but given up hope that I'd ever walk down the wedding aisle again.

Steve and I met in church. He came up to me one day and said he had been asked by my publisher to write some press releases on a book I had written. He wondered if we could meet for lunch. I told him that my publisher had neglected to tell me anything about him!

He was sweetly persistent, so I told him to call me at home after I had a chance to call the publisher. By the time I got home from church, he had called and left a message on my answering machine. I did verify that he was hired to do the press releases; I did have lunch with him; I did marry him a little over a year later.

It happens—and it can happen to you. You are not a statistic. No matter what your age or circumstances, God may intend for you to remarry. Until then, relax and live well.

"What Does the Future *Hold*?"

FEED ON HOPE

Without hope, we perish.

As you face the future, feed your spirit by continually returning to God and his Word. Sit with him, wait on him, struggle with him, pray, read, talk with other believers. Hope.

> *Now faith is being sure of what we hope for and*
> *certain of what we do not see.*
>
> HEBREWS 11:1

> *"For I know the plans I have for you," declares the*
> *LORD, "plans to prosper you and not to harm you,*
> *plans to give you hope and a future."*
>
> JEREMIAH 29:11

Praise be to the God and Father of our Lord Jesus
Christ! In his great mercy he has given us new birth
into a living hope through the resurrection of Jesus
Christ from the dead, and into an inheritance that
can never perish, spoil or fade—kept in heaven for
you, who through faith are shielded by God's power
until the coming of the salvation that is ready to be
revealed in the last time.

1 PETER 1:3-5

GOD IS FAITHFUL

My two-year-old grandson, Alex, has observed some of the worshipers in the church services he attends with his parents and brother. As a result he enthusiastically runs around with his arms up in the air saying, "Al-lu-ya," his version of "Hallelujah." He grins and waves his arms with little understanding of what his gestures mean. But I think he has gotten the message. Sometimes God's blessing so fills us that our praise spills out in words and songs and gestures.

Our certainty of God's presence and his love for us can carry us through difficulties. It can also enhance our good times with the awareness that they are his gifts.

When the future looks uncertain, remember that God is faithful and will continue to bless you.

> *I know whom I have believed, and am convinced*
> *that he is able to guard what I have entrusted to*
> *him for that day.*
>
> 2 TIMOTHY 1:12

MORE SWEET THAN BITTER

"What do you have there, Justin?" I asked my five-year-old grandson.

"My treasures from my Grandpa-Jack-in-heaven," he said as he spread out cuff links, tie tacks, and army brass insignias. The familiar men's brown jewelry box was open on the dining room table in front of Justin, who was scrutinizing each piece with special care.

I smiled as those old mementos brought back sweet memories: the day I pinned Jack's lieutenant's bars on his uniform, the cuff links that were a much-saved-for Christmas present, the monogrammed tie tack that he wore the night he received an insurance award.

"Do you remember these, Nana?" Justin looked up at me and asked.

"Oh yes, honey," I said, dry-eyed. "I remember."

Some memories fade, but most reside forever in a safe, lovely place in your heart. As time passes, those memories will become more sweet than bitter. You will still feel a tug or wipe away a tear, but you will be smiling too.

A RICH, FULL LIFE

This past year, Steve and I were visiting his family's home in Ohio. One Sunday after church we gave his Great-aunt Mid a ride home. Aunt Mid is ninety-seven years old and has been widowed for many years. She lives by herself in a cozy one-bedroom bungalow in an assisted-living community. Her garden next to the porch lies dormant in the winter cold, but she pointed out where her plants would come to life in the spring.

As we visited with her, she showed us her latest oil paintings and the stack of novels she's reading. She speaks lovingly of family still alive and those who are gone. Aunt Mid's life is full. She is a joy to be around and a model for the kind of woman we all could be.

No matter how long we live, or how much of that time we are alone, we can still live rich, full lives.

CLING TO HIM

When Jesus is in our lives, we live, even though our bodies may die. When he's not in our lives, we die, even though our bodies may live. Whatever pain or loss or tragedy we suffer, Jesus suffers with us and helps us endure.

Jesus holds your future in his hands and his heart. Nothing, not even death, can separate you from your Father, because his Son has given you eternal life. He makes the difference between despair and hope.

Cling to him.

Always.

> *My purpose is that they may be encouraged in heart*
> *and united in love, so that they may have the full*
> *riches of complete understanding, in order that they*
> *may know the mystery of God, namely, Christ, in*
> *whom are hidden all the treasures of wisdom and*
> *knowledge.*

COLOSSIANS 2:2-3

THE WONDER OF HEALING

Many years ago I hurt my knee in a skiing accident. After surgery, the pain continued for some time but lessened with every passing day. Now remnants of that accident remind me that I was badly wounded. When I exercise a lot or when the weather is particularly damp, my knee aches a little. But only a little. It is just enough to cause me to rejoice that I can walk and run and even ski. My knee is healed.

The same is true for my heart, which was dealt a near fatal blow when Jack was killed. My heart is now healed. Oh, I still feel a moment of slight pain now and then, but I can rejoice in the middle of that moment.

The healing took place at the hand of the Great Physician. Even though there are questions I cannot answer, I believe in the goodness of God. And my healing is the result of many years of trust that our God is a loving and kind God, despite the pain of loss.

God will heal you, too. In the middle of your pain, trust him for that healing and believe that it will come to pass. It *will* happen to you, if you yield to him daily. Cry out, wait, follow, cry out again, keep breathing, wait, and continue to follow. Trust, believe…no matter how you feel. One step at a time, just keep on keeping on with Jesus.

And one day you will realize that your heart is healed. You will rejoice.

The LORD is my strength and my shield;
my heart trusts in him, and I am helped.

My heart leaps for joy
and I will give thanks to him in song.

PSALM 28:7

GOD WILL WORK THINGS
OUT FOR YOUR GOOD

I couldn't stand it when people would come up to me and spout off the familiar words of Romans 8:28: "And we know that in all things God works for the good of those who love him, who have been called according to his purpose."

I know you know what I mean.

We believe that verse, but it stings when those words are flung at us as if to snap us out of our grief. It takes time to see goodness in our lives again, and we may never understand why God allowed our husbands to die. We may not be able to answer in our own hearts just how death can demonstrate anything good.

But many months after Jack died, I could once again look at that verse and receive the comfort it holds. There is a bigger picture than the one we see at any given moment, and God is working in all the moments of our lives. Time must pass and healing must happen before we can transform our belief in God's goodness into a reality in our lives.

God is patient, and he will stay beside you as you walk from grief to joy. Right now he is working those good things out in your life. Stay close to him.

Additional Scriptures for Comfort, Inspiration, and Instruction

Psalm 4:8

I will lie down and sleep in peace, for you alone, O LORD, make me dwell in safety.

Psalm 16:7-11

I will praise the Lord, who counsels me; even at night my heart instructs me. I have set the Lord always before me. Because he is at my right hand, I will not be shaken. Therefore my heart is glad and my tongue rejoices; my body also will rest secure, because you will not abandon me to the grave, nor will you let your Holy One see decay. You have made known to me the path of life; you will fill me with joy in your presence, with eternal pleasures at your right hand.

Psalm 17:8

Keep me as the apple of your eye; hide me in the shadow of your wings.

Psalm 18:33

He makes my feet like the feet of a deer; he enables me to stand on the heights.

Psalm 20:7

Some trust in chariots and some in horses, but we trust in the name of the LORD our God.

Psalm 27:8

My heart says of you, "Seek his face!" Your face, LORD, I will seek.

Psalm 27:13-14

I am still confident of this: I will see the goodness of the LORD in the land of the living. Wait for the LORD; be strong and take heart and wait for the LORD.

Psalm 28:7

The LORD is my strength and my shield; my heart trusts in him, and I am helped. My heart leaps for joy and I will give thanks to him in song.

Psalm 30:2

O LORD my God, I called to you for help and you healed me.

Psalm 30:11-12

You turned my wailing into dancing; you removed my sackcloth and clothed me with joy, that my heart may sing to you and not be silent. O LORD my God, I will give you thanks forever.

Psalm 34:3-4

Glorify the LORD with me; let us exalt his name together. I sought the LORD, and he answered me; he delivered me from all my fears.

Psalm 34:8

Taste and see that the LORD is good; blessed is the man who takes refuge in him.

Psalm 34:18

The LORD is close to the brokenhearted and saves those who are crushed in spirit.

Psalm 37:3-6

Trust in the LORD and do good; dwell in the land and enjoy safe pasture. Delight yourself in the LORD and he will give you the desires of your heart. Commit your way to the LORD; trust in him and he will do this: He will make your righteousness shine like the dawn, the justice of your cause like the noonday sun.

Psalm 40:2
He lifted me out of the slimy pit, out of the mud and mire; he set my feet on a rock and gave me a firm place to stand.

Psalm 46:1-3
God is our refuge and strength, an ever-present help in trouble. Therefore we will not fear, though the earth give way and the mountains fall into the heart of the sea, though its waters roar and foam and the mountains quake with their surging.

Psalm 46:10
Be still and know that I am God.

Psalm 51:10-12
Create in me a pure heart, O God, and renew a steadfast spirit within me. Do not cast me from your presence or take your Holy Spirit from me. Restore to me the joy of your salvation and grant me a willing spirit, to sustain me.

Psalm 84:11-12
For the LORD God is a sun and shield; the LORD bestows favor and

honor; no good thing does he withhold from those whose walk is blameless. O LORD Almighty, blessed is the man who trusts in you.

Proverbs 2:7-8
He holds victory in store for the upright, he is a shield to those whose walk is blameless, for he guards the course of the just and protects the way of his faithful ones.

Proverbs 3:5-6
Trust in the LORD with all your heart and lean not on your own understanding; in all your ways acknowledge him, and he will make your paths straight.

Isaiah 26:3
You will keep in perfect peace him whose mind is steadfast, because he trusts in you.

Isaiah 43:19
See, I am doing a new thing! Now it springs up; do you not perceive it? I am making a way in the desert and streams in the wasteland.

Jeremiah 29:11
"For I know the plans I have for you," declares the LORD, "plans to

prosper you and not to harm you, plans to give you hope and a future."

Jeremiah 33:3
Call to me and I will answer you and tell you great and unsearchable things you do not know.

John 1:12
Yet to all who received him, to those who believed in his name, he gave the right to become children of God.

Romans 4:3
Abraham believed God, and it was credited to him as righteousness.

Romans 4:20-21
Yet he [Abraham] did not waver through unbelief regarding the promise of God, but was strengthened in his faith and gave glory to God, being fully persuaded that God had power to do what he had promised.

Romans 5:8
But God demonstrates his own love for us in this: While we were still sinners, Christ died for us.

Romans 8:18

I consider that our present sufferings are not worth comparing with the glory that will be revealed in us.

Romans 8:24-25

For in this hope we were saved. But hope that is seen is no hope at all. Who hopes for what he already has? But if we hope for what we do not yet have, we wait for it patiently.

Romans 8:37-39

No, in all these things we are more than conquerors through him who loved us. For I am convinced that neither death nor life, neither angels nor demons, neither the present nor the future, nor any powers, neither height nor depth, nor anything else in all creation, will be able to separate us from the love of God that is in Christ Jesus our Lord.

1 Corinthians 2:9

However, as it is written: "No eye has seen, no ear has heard, no mind has conceived what God has prepared for those who love him."

2 Corinthians 3:18

And we, who with unveiled faces all reflect the Lord's glory, are being transformed into his likeness with ever-increasing glory, which comes from the Lord, who is the Spirit.

2 Corinthians 4:8-10
We are hard pressed on every side, but not crushed; perplexed, but not in despair; persecuted, but not abandoned; struck down, but not destroyed. We always carry around in our body the death of Jesus, so that the life of Jesus may also be revealed in our body.

2 Corinthians 4:18
So we fix our eyes not on what is seen, but on what is unseen. For what is seen is temporary, but what is unseen is eternal.

2 Corinthians 12:9
But he said to me, "My grace is sufficient for you, for my power is made perfect in weakness."

Ephesians 1:18-19
I pray also that the eyes of your heart may be enlightened in order that you may know the hope to which he has called you, the riches of his glorious inheritance in the saints, and his incomparably great power for us who believe.

Philippians 1:9-11

And this is my prayer: that your love may abound more and more in knowledge and depth of insight, so that you may be able to discern what is best and may be pure and blameless until the day of Christ, filled with the fruit of righteousness that comes through Jesus Christ—to the glory and praise of God.

Philippians 4:9

Whatever you have learned or received or heard from me, or seen in me—put it into practice. And the God of peace will be with you.

Philippians 4:11-13

I have learned to be content whatever the circumstances. I know what it is to be in need, and I know what it is to have plenty. I have learned the secret of being content in any and every situation, whether well fed or hungry, whether living in plenty or in want. I can do everything through him who gives me strength.

2 Timothy 1:7

For God did not give us a spirit of timidity, but a spirit of power, of love and of self-discipline.

2 Timothy 4:7-8

I have fought the good fight, I have finished the race, I have kept the faith. Now there is in store for me the crown of righteousness, which the Lord, the righteous Judge, will award to me on that day—and not only to me, but also to all who have longed for his appearing.

Hebrews 4:14-16

Therefore, since we have a great high priest who has gone through the heavens, Jesus the Son of God, let us hold firmly to the faith we profess. For we do not have a high priest who is unable to sympathize with our weaknesses, but we have one who has been tempted in every way, just as we are—yet was without sin. Let us then approach the throne of grace with confidence, so that we may receive mercy and find grace to help us in our time of need.

Hebrews 10:23

Let us hold unswervingly to the hope we profess, for he who promised is faithful.

Hebrews 10:35-37

So do not throw away your confidence; it will be richly rewarded. You need to persevere so that when you have done the will of God, you will receive what he has promised. For in just a very little while, "He who is coming will come and will not delay."

Hebrews 11:1
Now faith is being sure of what we hope for and certain of what we do not see.

Hebrews 13:15-16
Through Jesus, therefore, let us continually offer to God a sacrifice of praise—the fruit of lips that confess his name. And do not forget to do good and to share with others, for with such sacrifices God is pleased.

James 1:12
Blessed is the man who perseveres under trial, because when he has stood the test, he will receive the crown of life that God has promised to those who love him.

1 Peter 1:13
Therefore, prepare your minds for action; be self-controlled; set your hope fully on the grace to be given you when Jesus Christ is revealed.

1 Peter 4:12-13
Dear friends, do not be surprised at the painful trial you are suffering,

as though something strange were happening to you. But rejoice that you participate in the sufferings of Christ, so that you may be overjoyed when his glory is revealed.

1 Peter 5:7
Cast all your anxiety on him because he cares for you.

Revelation 21:1-5
Then I saw a new heaven and a new earth, for the first heaven and the first earth had passed away, and there was no longer any sea. I saw the Holy City, the new Jerusalem, coming down out of heaven from God, prepared as a bride beautifully dressed for her husband. And I heard a loud voice from the throne saying, "Now the dwelling of God is with men, and he will live with them. They will be his people, and God himself will be with them and be their God. He will wipe every tear from their eyes. There will be no more death or mourning or crying or pain, for the old order of things has passed away." He who was seated on the throne said, "I am making everything new!"